Hammond Oc

Happy Birthday, Dad!

Love,
Doug & Sally

*True Tales of
the Prairies and Plains*

Previous Books by David Dary

The Buffalo Book

True Tales of the Old-Time Plains

Cowboy Culture: A Saga of Five Centuries

Entrepreneurs of the Old West

Seeking Pleasure in the Old West

True Tales of Old-Time Kansas

More True Tales of Old-Time Kansas

Kanzana, 1854–1900: A Selected Bibliography of Books, Pamphlets, and Ephemera of Kansas

Lawrence, Douglas County, Kansas: An Informal History

Red Blood and Black Ink: Journalism in the Old West

Pictorial History of Lawrence, Kansas

The Santa Fe Trail: Its History, Legends, and Lore

The Oregon Trail: An American Saga

The Oklahoma Publishing Company's First Century: The Gaylord Family Story

A Texas Cowboy's Journal: Up the Trail to Kansas in 1868

DAVID DARY

True Tales of the Prairies and Plains

UNIVERSITY PRESS OF KANSAS

Published by the University Press of Kansas (Lawrence, Kansas 66045), which was organized
by the Kansas Board of Regents and is operated and funded by Emporia State University, Fort
Hays State University, Kansas State University, Pittsburg State University, the University of
Kansas, and Wichita State University

Library of Congress Cataloging-in-Publication Data

Dary, David.
    True tales of the prairies and plains / David Dary.
       p.   cm.
    Includes bibliographical references and index.
    ISBN-13: 978-0-7006-1518-6 (cloth : alk. paper)
    1. West (U.S.)—History—Anecdotes. 2. Great Plains—History—Anecdotes. 3. Prairies—
West (U.S.)—History—Anecdotes. 4. West (U.S.)—Social life and customs—Anecdotes.
5. Great Plains—Social life and customs—Anecdotes. 6. Frontier and pioneer life—West
(U.S.)—Anecdotes. 7. Frontier and pioneer life—Great Plains—Anecdotes. 8. Pioneers—West
(U.S.)—Biography—Anecdotes. 9. Pioneers—Great Plains—Biography—Anecdotes. I. Title.
    F591.D27 2007
    978--dc22   2006037913

British Library Cataloguing-in-Publication Data is available.

Printed in the United States of America

10 9 8 7 6 5 4 3 2 1

The paper used in this publication meets the minimum requirements of the American National
Standard for Permanence of Paper for Printed Library Materials Z39.48-1992.

*For Sue, who has ridden the same trail with me for
more than half a century*

The Plains

Give me the plains,—the barren and sun-beaten plains!
Free in the vague indeterminate murmur of winds,
High on the arched and tremendous back of the world,
Alone and close up under the skies,
Let me lie dark in the grass like an Indian,
Hearing loud footfalls afar in the rumbling sod,
And know that it knows me!—Up from the grass to the sky,
From the skies again back to the grass—I go to the plains!

                                              —Maynard Dixon

The Prairies

I wonder indeed if the people of this continental inland West know how much of first-class *art* they have in these prairies—how original and all your own—how much of the influences of a character for your future humanity, broad, patriotic, heroic and new? how entirely they tally on land the grandeur and superb monotony of the skies of heaven and the ocean with its waters? how freeing, soothing, nourishing they are to the soul? . . . This favor'd central area of (in round numbers) two thousand miles square seems fated to be the home of both of what I would call America's distinctive ideas and distinctive realities.

                                              —Walt Whitman

CONTENTS

PART III   THE LAWLESS, LAWMEN, AND JUSTICE

PART IV   BUFFALO, HORSES, AND OTHER CREATURES

PART V   THE FAMOUS AND THE OBSCURE

PREFACE

This is a collection of stories set on the prairies and plains of middle America that stretch from the Rio Grande northward into Canada. As one who was born in this region and still calls it home, the land exerts a peaceful if not calming influence. Many natives say the same, but each usually favors their home area because it is where their roots are deepest. Whether someone's home is Texas, with its mild climate, or in the north, where winters are harsh, most people native to the prairies and plains savor the wide-open spaces, the broad horizons and memorable sunsets, and those clear nights when millions of stars dot the moonless sky. These things tie everyone in the region to the land and their maker.

First-time visitors to the prairies and plains are often struck by the vast distances between the larger cities and what many describe as the "nothingness" between the watering holes. As newcomers drive across the region on interstate highways, some complain about the flatness of the land or the lack of trees and vegetation. Some complain that the openness makes them feel uncomfortable, as if they were not in control of their destiny. Such complaints usually come from people raised in large eastern cities, where signs of human civilization are everywhere. For many of these outsiders, the prairies and plains are simply something that must be crossed to reach somewhere else. These visitors rarely get off the interstate highways. When they do, many are surprised to find nice towns with comfortable homes. They find farms and ranches, as well as trees and rolling hills that sometimes remind them of New England, or of the Appalachians, but without forests. The outsiders meet people who prefer life on the plains and prairies to living in crowded cities choked with heavy traffic and bad air, where people live in apartment buildings or expensive cookie-cutter houses in subdivisions with names that suggest peace, tranquility, and isolation, all designed to erase the reality of overcrowding. But most persons living on the plains and prairies know this and hope the multitudes will not discover their paradise in middle America. As one eastern transplant commented a few years ago, "Life on the plains and prairies is America's best-kept secret."

The stereotyped dullness of the plains and prairies often portrayed by outsiders also ignores the region's colorful history, the spirit of the people who were there before the white man, and the spirit of the pioneers who moved west to settle the land. Certainly the history of the prairies and plains contains many pages filled with excitement and romance, but more often, because of the land, the story includes the feelings of peace and tranquility in living close to nature. The western plains and prairies are a far cry from the man-made caverns of big cities, the rolling forested country, or the deserts found elsewhere in America.

The stories between these two covers seek to capture some of the history, romance, and adventure of early life on the plains and prairie. Some stories are exciting and colorful; others convey the slow feeling of grass growing. Regardless, they reflect the reality of life on the early western plains and prairies during the nineteenth and early twentieth centuries.

*True Tales of
the Prairies and Plains*

Prairie and Plains Region

CANADA

MONTANA
36

NORTH DAKOTA
29 10 39

MN

SOUTH DAKOTA
3 27
32 35
23

20 38
10

WYOMING

NEBRASKA

IA

11

38 33 8
37

COLORADO

KANSAS
38 8
28 31
28
13 25
15 7
34
12 6 21
5 27

MO

30
4
27

9 17
16
22

OKLAHOMA
38

12 19

AR

NEW MEXICO

2

14

MEXICO

24
18

TEXAS
5

LA

GULF OF MEXICO

(Courtesy International Programs, U.S. Department of State)

MAP KEY

Numbers on map key correspond to location of numbered stories below. Where a number appears more than once, the story occurred in more than one location.

Part I

OVER THE TRAILS AND RAILS

The thing to remember when traveling is that the trail is the thing,
not the end of the trail. Travel too fast and you miss all you are traveling for.
—Louis L'Amour

1

Jim Fugate's Adventures on the Santa Fe Trail

It was a sunny spring day on May 21, 1853, when the long line of freight wagons halted in the Arkansas River Valley near where Hutchinson, Kansas, stands today. The fifty-seven men made camp and began to prepare their midday meal, which they called "dinner." As they sat down to eat, someone yelled, "Indians!" Everyone looked where he pointed. On the horizon, the men saw about two hundred mounted Cheyenne charging toward their wagons. The teamsters quickly moved their wagons into a defensive circle and prepared for battle. As the Indians neared the wagons, the teamsters could hear them yell. Some Indians fired rifles. Others shot arrows toward the wagons, which were heavily laden with trading goods bound for Santa Fe.

We know what happened that spring day because one of the teamsters, young James M. Fugate, later wrote his recollections. "Taken by such a dangerous disadvantage and surprise, we were just in that position which makes men fight with desperation, and instantaneously our rifles were pealing forth their notes of defiance and death to the murderous foe."

The wagon train, with forty-five men under the command of J. W. Jones, had left Lexington in Lafayette County, Missouri, east of modern Kansas City, Missouri, about a month earlier. Their journey was uneventful as the wagon train crossed into what months later would be Kansas Territory and headed down the Santa Fe Trail to Council Grove, the last settlement before reaching New Mexico. Many miles west of Council Grove, the wagon train came on twelve Santa Fe–bound men with three wagons waiting along the trail. They said they had heard of Indian trouble ahead. Knowing there was safety in numbers, they had decided to wait and join other traders going to Santa Fe. The dozen men and their three wagons joined the larger train, and everyone headed down the trail.

Jim Fugate remembered that as the Indians began circling the wagons, they swung to the opposite side of their ponies, "exposing but little of themselves to our aim by firing under the horses' necks. Their deadly missiles were soon playing havoc among our cattle. The poor creatures were madly surging and bellowing around, endangering us to a death beneath their feet, worse to be feared within the enclosure than the foe without. This new danger soon drove us outside the enclosure of wagons in full view of the Indians."

As Fugate and the others moved outside the corral of wagons, the Indians narrowed their circle. Riding within about twenty-five yards of the wagons, the motion of their ponies unsteadied their aim until it was but random. Fugate and the others found that as the Indians pressed nearer, the teamsters became more destructive with every shot they fired. Realizing their rifles were not very effective, the Indians quickly turned to using their bows and arrows.

Fugate tells us what happened next:

> Finding themselves getting most terribly worsted in the combat, they made a dash to ride down and tomahawk us all in one death struggle. I tell you, then, we had no child's play. Outnumbered four or five to one in a hand-to-hand fight to death, is a serious thing. We were soon mingling together, but driven against the wagons, we could dodge or parry their blows with the tomahawk, while the rapid flashes from the celebrate "navy" in each man's hand [probably a Colt Navy Model 1851 percussion revolver], was not so easily avoided by the savage warriors. We made the ground too hot for them, and with yells of baffled rage, they broke and fled, carrying off all of their killed and wounded but three, which they had to leave.

Fugate and the others looked around to evaluate their situation. One of the teamsters, a young man named Gilbert, was dead. His revolver had misfired. He had picked up a rifle and was using it as a club against the Indians when he died. Fugate remembered that Gilbert "lay as he fell, with his hand clenched around the stock of his gun as though he would take the weapon with his departed spirit to the other world." Many other teamsters were wounded, two seriously. Outside the corral of wagons, "dead and dying ponies were scattered about on the prairie with the arms and accouterments of their savage owners about them, while several of our cattle were also dead and dying from wounds made by missiles aimed for us," recalled Fugate.

Fugate and the other uninjured teamsters spent the afternoon burying Gilbert's body on the spot, taking care of the wounded, and gathering up the spoils of the fight. "We destroyed everything belonging to the Indians that we could not carry away," Fugate remembered. Toward dusk, the teamsters moved their wagons and their wounded about one mile away to the bank of the Arkansas River and made camp. After an evening meal, the men, except those on guard, sat around the campfires talking. Fugate wrote that they talked over their chances of reaching New Mexico with their small force. "The future looked hopeless indeed, but J. W. Jones who commanded the outfit, swore he could go to Santa Fe, or go to hell. We dared not show the white feather, then."

By dawn the next morning, the teamsters were breaking camp and moving toward the trail. The slow journey was uneventful until late in the afternoon as they neared Walnut Creek, a tributary of the Arkansas River. There they made camp in a horseshoe bend on the west side of the creek. The night was peaceful, but at dawn, as the guards were taking the oxen out of the corral to graze, perhaps as many as five hundred Cheyenne appeared. Some were mounted on ponies; others were on foot. The Indians wanted to steal the oxen.

"At the east end the Indians broke through and came into the corral, but of those who came through it is a question if any ever returned. They were immediately shot and clubbed with the guns. I broke my own gunstock over the head of one of the miscreants. There were nine of them left with the corral dead. The Indians, seeing the fate that had befallen their comrades who went through under the wagons, began a hasty retreat, and were quickly followed by the entire pack as fast as they could run. They took refuge in a low range of sand hills along the Arkansas River, some 60 or 80 rods to the south, from which they emerged occasionally during the morning to harass us." Fugate said that he and the others followed the Indians toward the sand hills, firing at them, but when the teamsters got as far as the low sag, they retreated to the safety of the corralled wagons. There the wagon master, J. W. Jones, counted the bodies of sixty dead Indians inside and outside their corral of wagons. Five teamsters had been killed and several wounded, and a few of them would later die of their injuries.

All was quiet until about midmorning, when the men in the corral saw another party of armed white men forming a line to the west and moving toward the Indians. Fugate and the others soon learned the armed white men were from another wagon train owned by Majors & Russell of Missouri, camped about a half mile to the west. Seeing them moving toward the Indians, Fugate and the other teamsters in his train left their corral to join them, and soon all of them were moving together toward the Indians. It was then that the Indians beat a hasty retreat across the Arkansas River.

Fugate and the teamsters from his train apparently visited with the teamsters from the other train and thanked them for their help. The teamsters then returned to their respective camps. At Fugate's camp, he and others buried the dead on a point between two draws a little ways southwest of their camp. At about two o'clock that afternoon, they broke camp and soon joined the Majors & Russell wagon train and continued down the Santa Fe Trail. About five or six miles down the trail, the teamsters had a brush with more Indians, but nothing serious occurred until early the next afternoon, when they camped about 200 yards south of Pawnee Rock. The night passed without incident, but the following morning, at about eight o'clock, just as the oxen were being yoked, a band of about three hundred Cheyenne suddenly charged the wagons from the north around both sides of Pawnee Rock.

"Leaving our cattle just as they were, some yoked, some partly yoked, we instantly seized our weapons and pitched in vigorously to repulse the assault," wrote Fugate. "The Indians opened a heavy fire from the start. They made strainers of our wagon-boxes by perforating them with bullets and arrowheads. The Indians who were mounted fired high, and many [may have] hit some of their own men on the opposite side of the corral. After firing in this way for a while, and finding they could gain nothing, they beat a hasty retreat to the south, taking with them their dead and wounded, who were in nearly all cases tied to their ponies, as was shown by the thongs that lay by some of the dead ponies, where the riders had cut loose and got away."

In that fight at Pawnee Rock, one teamster was wounded and several oxen were killed. The next morning, the wagon train continued down the trail. Fugate remembered that they had to fight Indians every few days. "We had engagements at Pawnee Fork, again near [Fort] Dodge, again at Cimarron, and at Mount Aubrey," in what is now Kearney County, Kansas. When Fugate and the others reached Mount Aubrey, they found a party of eleven Spaniards who had been attacked by Indians. Ten of them were dead; the eleventh was still alive but had been scalped, and he died a few hours after he was found.

The wagon train camped near where the Spaniards had been attacked. The night passed peacefully, but at first light, a band of Kiowa-Apaches and Arapahos attacked. Fugate remembered that they "first fired on the guards, and then coming up by slow, cautious movements, seeking every buffalo-wallow, or other slight protection to cover themselves. So stealthily and-steadily did they advance that almost before we were aware of it we had eight men lying dead. All this time we kept up a vigorous and pointed fire, always aiming and firing with intent to kill. About ten o'clock, finding they could not capture our train, they retreated the way they came, leaving their dead on the ground. These, amounting to between 50 and 80, we piled up on the plains, and left for the coyotes and buzzards."

The wagon train remained in camp for four days. They buried their dead, including the Spaniards. To pass the time, Fugate recalled, "we amused ourselves at target-shooting, using for a target the head of some luckless Indian, which would be placed in all conceivable positions to be shot at. We had some more fighting now and then until we reached Fort Bent, after which we were out of hostile country, and reached Santa Fe in safety, with what we had left of men and animals. We lost no wagons, and carried our cargo entirely through."

2

How the Staked Plains
Got Their Name

On October 20, 1541, Spanish explorer Francisco Vázquez de Coronado and his party came upon a vast region of plains that today cover all or part of thirty-three counties in west Texas and four in New Mexico, an area larger than all of New England. Coronado called the region the *Llano Estacado*, which in English means "Staked Plains." That day Coronado sent a letter to the King of Spain in which he noted, "I reached some plains so vast, that I did not find their limit anywhere I went, although I traveled over them for more than 300 leagues . . . with no more landmarks than if we had been swallowed up by the sea. There was not a stone, nor bit of rising ground, nor a tree, nor a shrub, nor anything to go by." This is the earliest known description of the Staked Plains, the southern extension of the Great Plains of central North America that covers about 32,000 square miles. Coronado and members of his expedition viewed the Staked Plains as desolate and isolated. Physically, they are set apart from the rest of the Great Plains on the north by the Canadian River and from the more humid lower plains to the east by the Caprock escarpment. To the southwest, the Staked Plains are separated from arid southwestern New Mexico by the Mescalero Escarpment. The Staked Plains merge directly only with the Edward Plateau to the south.

8

In Coronado's day, countless buffalo, pronghorn antelope, gray wolves, grizzly bear, and elk could be found on the Staked Plains. Shallow lakes called *playas* by Coronado dotted the region. (When *playa* is translated into English, it means "beach.") Why Coronado did not use the words *laquito* or *lagito,* meaning "little lake," is not known. The sandy soils of the Staked Plains supported a thick growth of low shin oak, mesquite, and sand sage. Along the rivers and streams, they probably found cottonwood and willow trees. The Spaniards found a sea of grass, which was still there about three hundred years later when U.S. Army Captain Randolph B. Marcy explored the region and described it as "generally a very short variety of mesquite, called buffalo-grass, from one to two inches in length, and gives the plains the appearance of an interminable meadow that has been recently mown very close to the earth."

Captain Marcy, who first crossed the region in 1849, described the Staked Plains as "the great Zahara of North America" and noted that it "must continue uninhabited forever." Marcy, however, had no way of knowing that Apaches had used the region extensively until the middle 1700s, when Comanches forced them to leave. *Comancheros,* as the New Mexico Indian traders were called, *pastores* (sheepherders), and *ciboleros* (buffalo hunters) used the Staked Plains extensively until the 1870s. When *ciboleros* hunted buffalo in the region, they stuck poles in the ground and between them stretched lines on which they hung slabs of buffalo meat to dry. Therefore, so as not to lose their way on the flat plains, Ciboleros used buffalo bones or yucca stems to stake a route that would lead them back to camp after hunting or to water.

The white man did not begin to take up residence on the Staked Plains until the 1870s, when cattle ranchers discovered the region's free grass and water. One was Charles Goodnight, who in the middle 1870s settled in Palo Duro Canyon, south of modern Amarillo, Texas. He claimed that he had to drive thousands of buffalo out of Palo Duro Canyon in order to make room for his cattle. For untold decades, buffalo had found refuge during the winter months in the canyon, which probably gave rise to the belief of many Indians on the southern plains that buffalo came up out of the earth, and therefore, they originated there.

The first settlers on the Staked Plains were members of a Quaker colony called Estacado in what is today Crosby County, Texas. The leader of the colony, Paris Cox, had come west from Indiana to hunt buffalo and liked the country. He went east, got his wife and family, and returned to Texas in 1876, where he secured authority to sell land to settlers at twenty-five cents an acre. Some of the families who joined Cox found the winter too difficult and returned to the East, but the following year, more friends and relatives arrived. By the summer of 1881, the colony comprised ten families. The community of Estacado flourished until 1888, when Cox died.

In the meantime, other cattle ranchers had moved onto the Staked Plains, and by the late 1880s, at least thirty large ranches had been established. Until supply centers could be set up, most of the ranchers' supplies were brought into the region by wagons from Dodge City, Kansas. However, during a six-year period beginning in 1874, three towns were founded in the northern area of the Staked Plains. Mobeetie was first in 1874. It evolved from a supply store on Sweetwater Creek, located at a buffalo hunters' camp called Hidetown and a settlement for sheepherders called Plaza Atascosa located on the Canadian River. In 1876, the settlement was renamed Tascosa. The third town was Clarendon, located at the junction of Carroll Creek and the Salt Fork on the Red River, founded as a Methodist community in the fall of 1878. Unlike Tascosa and Mobeetie, Clarendon had no bars, and at one point, it counted seven Methodist ministers as residents. No wonder that many residents of the Staked Plains referred to Clarendon as the "Saint's Roost." By 1880, the whole population of the Staked Plains, including the residents of the three towns, was only a little over one thousand humans and an untold number of cattle.

Why Coronado named the vast region *Llano Estacado*, or "Staked Plains," is still a matter of speculation. Accounts of Coronado's expedition mention "stakes" but are unclear about what they were. Occasionally there is reference to "piles of bones and cow dung" being used as markers. Some people believe that when the Spanish first saw the region, they could not help but notice the stockadelike appearance of the geologic formations that form its boundaries—hence staked, or stockade, plains. Others speculate that the name came from the long, straight stalks of the yucca plants found in the region. Another belief held by some is that Llano Estacado is a transformation of the original name, *Llano Estrancado*, which means "Plain of

Many Ponds." Still others, perhaps looking for a more practical answer, credit the name to the fact that early Spaniards had to push marker sticks in the ground along their path as they moved through the featureless region, or that the Spanish had to place stakes in the ground as ties for their horses because the region had nothing to permit this, except along the rivers and streams.

Although the origin of the name still remains a mystery, old-timers on the Staked Plains seem to agree that the western phrase "wide open spaces" was probably coined on the Staked Plains by an early traveler.

3

The Ride of "Portugee" John Phillips

One thing is certain; of all the monuments which the Spaniard
has left to glorify his reign in America there will be none more
worthy than his horse. . . . The Spaniard's horse may be found
today in countless thousands, from the city of Montezumas to the
regions of perpetual snow; they are grafted into our equine
wealth and make an important impression on the horse of the
country.

These words were written by artist Frederic Remington in 1888 for
an article published in *Century* magazine. Until the arrival of the railroad and later the horseless carriage, mules, oxen, and horses provided people with mobility. Of these, the horse was far more than
simply a beast of burden. Charles Goodnight, the father of the Texas
Panhandle, once wrote, "man and horse were one, and the combination accomplished feats that would be utterly impossible under ordi-
nary circumstances."

This tale of the ride of "Portugee" John Phillips and a blooded
Kentucky runner ranks in heroism above the legendary ride of Paul
Revere. It occurred in 1866, when men were heading to the new
goldfields of Idaho and Montana, and they were crossing land claimed
by the Indians. The government in Washington ordered the U.S.

12

John "Portugee" Phillips arriving at Horseshoe Station, where word of the Fetterman massacre and Colonel Carrington's plea for help was sent over the telegraph. Phillips, however, did not trust the telegraph and rode on to Fort Laramie, arriving on Christmas Eve 1866. Artist unknown. (Courtesy Western History Collections, University of Oklahoma Libraries)

Army to build a string of forts along the Bozeman Trail to protect the emigrants from the Sioux and a few Arapahoe and Cheyenne Indians threatening the gold seekers.

The Bozeman Trail began at Fort Laramie and ran north on the plains, along the eastern edge of the Big Horn Mountains in present-day Wyoming. It crossed the Big Horn River in what is today southern Montana, and west to Virginia City. It was a fast trail. There were few streams to cross, and it was well watered and grassed, but it was through Sioux country.

Colonel Henry Beebe Carrington was ordered to build the forts. When he set out from Fort Laramie, one of the new posts was Fort Phil Kearny on the banks of Piney Creek, a branch of the Powder River. The fort was named for General Philip Kearny, a Civil War hero.

Between August and early December 1866, Indians made fifty-one attacks in the vicinity of Fort Phil Kearny, but the post was not besieged. Each day, a wood train managed to go out to find timber to construct the fort, and supply trains came and went with little difficulty. But about eleven o'clock on the morning of December 21, 1866, the post lookout reported that the wood train was being attacked by Indians. Captain William J. Fetterman led a relief party from the post to save the wood train. Against orders, Fetterman pursued the Indians over Lodge Trail Ridge along the Bozeman Trail.

It was a trap.

Within a short time every man in the relief party was killed, but the wood train returned to the safety of the fort, as did Portugee John Phillips, a civilian, who was engaged in hauling water to fill the post's barrels at the time the wood train was attacked. Phillips was born Manual Felipe Cardoso on the island of Pico in the Azores in 1832. A citizen of Portugal by birth, he came to America aboard a whaling ship bound for California. The eighteen-year-old spent the next fifteen years searching for gold in California and what is now Oregon, Idaho, Montana, and Wyoming, where he found work at Fort Phil Kearny.

Phillips was at the post on the afternoon of the massacre, when the bodies of forty-nine men were recovered. Late that afternoon, the weather began to change. The temperature dropped rapidly, and a blizzard soon began. Snow started to pile up against the walls of the stockade. Efforts to recover more bodies stopped. By nightfall, the snowdrifts were so high along the stockade's wall that details of men were constantly shoveling it away. Colonel Carrington feared the Indians might attack: they would be able to simply climb the snowdrifts to the top of the stockade walls and jump inside.

At about nine o'clock that night, the temperature stood near thirty below zero. The cold was so intense that sentries remained on guard duty for only twenty minutes at a time. Even with quick relief, however, many a man received frozen fingers, feet, nose, and ears. Colonel Carrington knew the greatly reduced garrison must get help. And he knew the outside world must be told of the massacre, but there was no telegraph at the fort. The nearest telegraph was at Horseshoe Station, more than two hundred miles away, near Fort Laramie. Carrington knew he must send a messenger.

The colonel called for volunteers. At first, no one volunteered. A handful of old plainsmen, some scouts, and the veteran soldiers shook their heads. They did not want to go. They knew a ride to Fort Laramie through the cold and snow would mean almost certain death. And if the cold did not kill the rider and his horse, certainly the Indians would.

It was then, to the surprise of many, that a swarthy man in his middle thirties, tough and wiry of frame, said he would go. It was

Phillips—nicknamed "Portugee" because of his native land—who volunteered. It is unclear why he did so. It may have been the challenge and thrill of danger or the desire to help his comrades. Or it may have been the fact that there were a few women and children at the fort, the families of some of the officers.

One of the women was Frances Grummond, the widow of Lieutenant Grummond, one of the officers killed in the massacre. She would later write that Phillips was moved by sorrow for her and by tender emotion. The story is told in her book *My Army Life*. Mrs. Grummond later became Colonel Carrington's second wife and wrote the book in 1910 as Frances C. Carrington.

On volunteering, Phillips asked to have the best horse at the fort for the ride. Colonel Carrington quickly agreed and gave Phillips his beautiful black horse with Kentucky blood, the swiftest animal at the post. The horse's name was Dandy. Carrington also gave Phillips a Spencer repeating rifle and one hundred rounds of ammunition. Phillips strapped the ammunition on his ankles to provide enough weight to keep his feet firmly in the stirrups.

Carrington quickly wrote two messages. One was addressed to General Phillip St. George Cooke in Omaha, asking for reinforcements and supplies and telling of the Fetterman massacre. The other message was addressed to General Ulysses S. Grant in Washington, telling of the massacre and asking for new Spencer repeating rifles.

Portugee Phillips prepared for the ride. Dressing as warmly as he could in a buffalo coat and several layers of clothing, Phillips slipped a few biscuits—hardtack—into his pockets. He tied a quarter sack of oats for his horse to the saddle. Then, leading the horse, Phillips joined Colonel Carrington and walked to the water gate at the southeast end of the quartermaster yard. A sergeant opened the gate. Carrington and Phillips walked through the gate with Phillips leading the horse. By then, another civilian at the post had volunteered to accompany Phillips. His name was Daniel Dixon.

For about a minute, as Dixon saddled his horse, Phillips and Carrington talked quietly. Then Phillips mounted Carrington's horse, and Dixon mounted his animal. Carrington was heard to tell Phillips and Dixon, "May God help you."

A soldier, John C. Brough, standing guard at the gate, later recalled that Phillips "wheeled and started on a trot. So did Dixon. For about thirty seconds we could hear the hoof beats, and then they ceased. Carrington stood with his head bent on one side, as if listening intently, and then straightening up and speaking to no one in particular, said, 'Good, they have taken softer ground at the side of the trail.'"

The exact route followed by Portugee Phillips and Dixon has been lost in time, but he chose not to ride through the timbered valleys or along the Bozeman Trail, where Indians stood watch. Instead, they followed the high, shelterless divides where it was colder, but where there was less snow and fewer Indians.

Several hours later, Phillips reached Fort Reno, a tiny outpost almost sixty-seven miles south of Fort Phil Kearny. There Phillips warmed himself, fed his horse, and told of the massacre. Dixon remained at Fort Reno, but Phillips soon left.

In the predawn darkness, Phillips mounted his horse and left Fort Reno, reportedly accompanied by another rider. At dawn, the two men sought shelter in a valley and hid all day among the trees. At dusk, the two men again set out for Horseshoe Station.

Traveling through what probably seemed like one continuous blizzard, riding only at night, rationing oats carefully to their horses and eating snow for water, Portugee Phillips and the other rider covered the one hundred thirty miles from Fort Reno to Horseshoe Station during the next two nights.

At Horseshoe Station, about forty miles north of Fort Laramie, Phillips handed the dispatches to the telegraph operator John Friend. The dispatches were transmitted. For some reason, however, Phillips did not trust the telegraph. He rebound his legs with sacks, wrapped himself in the buffalo coat, stuffed the dispatches in his pockets, and set out at about noon for Fort Laramie. Again, another unidentified rider from Horseshoe Station joined him.

It was nearly midnight on Christmas Eve when Portugee Phillips and the other rider reached Fort Laramie. Snow and ice matted Phillips's beard, and icicles were hanging from his buffalo coat. As the two riders passed through the gate, music could be heard coming from a large building called "Bedlam"—the post headquarters. A full-dress Christmas Eve garrison ball was being held.

Phillips told the officer of the guard that he had to see the commanding officer at once. The officer of the guard, likely shocked by

Phillips's appearance, must have sensed something important had happened and told Phillips to follow him. The commanding officer, he said, was at the ball.

As Phillips dismounted, his horse sank to the ground. Before Phillips returned, the animal died from cold and exhaustion. Portugee had not changed mounts during the entire 236-mile ride.

When the snow-covered figure of Phillips entered the ballroom, the music stopped. Everyone stared at Phillips. His eyebrows, crusted with ice and snow, were twice their normal size. He asked the commanding officer in a trembling voice if he had received the telegraph messages. The officer said he had, but that they were garbled. He had not understood them.

Slowly, his voice weak, Phillips told the story of the massacre and delivered the dispatches. Aid was sent to Fort Phil Kearny, and the post was saved.

It took Portugee Phillips many weeks to recover from his ordeal. Records show that Phillips was paid three hundred dollars by the government for the ride. The ride, however, supposedly cost him far more than the suffering he had experienced. One tale claims that Sioux Indians, upon learning of his ride, swore vengeance. Whether this is true is not known.

In December 1870, Phillips married Hattie Buck, a native of Indiana. They settled down on a ranch near modern Chugwater, Wyoming, north of Cheyenne. There, about six years after his ride, Indians attacked his ranch and killed all of his stock. Phillips soon sold his ranch and moved to Cheyenne, where on November 18, 1883, he died from a kidney infection and was buried in Lakeview Cemetery. He was about fifty-one years old.

In 1898, thirty-two years after his heroic ride, the government paid his solitary and destitute widow five thousand dollars to settle a claim against the Indian depredation on the ranch of the man who rode one horse 236 miles in four days through driving snow and freezing cold to bring help to Fort Phil Kearny.

4

The Texan Who Invaded New Mexico

It was in 1872 when forty-one-year-old John Nathan Hittson, a native of Tennessee, decided to put a stop to cattle rustling on the Staked Plains of West Texas. Hittson had lost too many cattle to Comanches who were in cahoots with some New Mexicans called Comancheros. Josiah Gregg coined the name about three decades earlier in his classic book *Commerce of the Prairies*, published in 1844. Gregg described the Comancheros as poor people from the villages of New Mexico "who collect together several times a year and launch upon the plains with a few trinkets and trumperies of all kinds" to trade with Comanches for stolen horses, mules, and cattle. The value of the trading stock of an individual Comanchero was seldom more than twenty dollars.

Comancheros came into being in 1786 when the Spanish governor of New Mexico made a treaty with the Comanches that allowed trade between New Mexicans and the Indians in exchange for protection against intruders on Spanish territory. The trade gradually grew until the Mexican War, when it slowed. During the 1850s, it resumed and grew to include whiskey, guns, lead, and powder. The trade further increased when Anglo ranchers moved onto the Staked Plains of West Texas and the market for Texas cattle and horses in New Mexico grew.

Newly arriving Anglo merchants and settlers in New Mexico seized on the trade to make more money and to stock new cattle ranches. Given the opportunity, some U.S. soldiers even found the trade to be profitable. Such was the case at Fort Bascom in northeast New Mexico, where officers relied on the Comancheros for horses and beef for the soldiers.

When ranchers like John Hittson moved onto the Staked Plains of West Texas soon after the Civil War, the increased number of cattle and horses provided more opportunities for the Indians. The increasing number of cattlemen on the Staked Plains experienced many skirmishes with the Indians. When John Hittson's ranch head-quarters was at Camp Cooper, an abandoned federal post in modern Throckmorton County, Texas, he experienced such a skirmish about noon on a warm June day. Hittson and his older brother, William, along with Jess Hittson (John's young son), two cowboys, and Free-man Ward, a former black slave, were rounding up cattle on Tecum-seh Creek, about three miles north of Camp Cooper. Suddenly a band of Indians attacked.

One of the two cowboys managed to escape, rushed to Camp Cooper, and reported that everyone else in the party had been killed. Such was not the case. Although the former slave was killed by the Indians, the Hittsons and the other cowboy managed to escape and rode more than a mile to a bluff along a small stream that emptied into Tecumseh Creek. They dismounted and sought cover in a small cave under the bluff. Soon Indians surrounded them. They fired ar-rows into the cave and rolled rocks toward the opening from above. One of the rocks knocked the sight off a rifle held by one of the men in the cave.

As the summer sun beat down on the cliff, the Indians fired many arrows into the cave. One arrow struck John Hittson in the thigh. In the meantime, the Indians killed the cowboys' horses. The Hittsons and the cowboys fired their weapons whenever they saw an Indian, but the warriors never tried to enter the cave. The men re-mained in the cave until dark. By then, the Indians had given up and ridden away, taking Hittson's cattle with them. The four men then walked back to Camp Cooper, where everyone, including the wives of John and William Hittson, were surprised but delighted to learn that the men had not been killed. John Hittson's wound was treated, and he recovered. The next morning, the Hittson brothers buried Freeman Ward on the spot where he died. During the next few years, John Hittson suffered major cattle losses to the Comanches, who traded the cattle to Comancheros, who in turn sold them in New Mexico. His losses soon became so great that in 1872, Hittson decided to put a stop to the cattle stealing. He obtained powers of attorney from a large number of Texas ranchers who had lost cattle to the Comanches.

Hittson then hired a group of armed cowboys. Some accounts suggest the number was fifty, but other accounts say there were nearly one hundred men. Hittson was determined to take his little army and invade New Mexico to recover cattle bearing Texas brands for which there were no bills of sale. Hugh Martin Childress Jr., a well-known West Texas cattle drover who supposedly had trailed more cattle than John Hittson, John Chisum, or Charles Goodnight, joined Hittson and his little army of cowboys, and they wept into New Mexico. They went from ranch to ranch along the Pecos near Las Vegas, New Mexico. At one stop, a rancher named Simpson told Hittson that he would not give up the cattle he had bought from the Comancheros. When Hittson's cowboys knocked down the poles at a gate to drive the cattle from the corral, Simpson blocked the gate. The cowboys shot him and drove the cattle out of the corral over Simpson's body.

John Hittson and his little army recovered about eleven thousand stolen cattle and three hundred stolen horses before legal difficulties prompted him to end his invasion of New Mexico. The cattle and horses were driven away and sold—one account says in Denver—but from what is known, none of the Texas ranchers whose cattle were recovered was ever reimbursed. Some accounts suggest that Hittson kept the money. Some of it was supposedly used by his sons-in-law to construct an office building in Denver. Although a few Texas cattlemen complained, in the end, Hittson's expenses invading New Mexico were probably as large as the value of the cattle recovered and sold.

The story of John Hittson reflects the rugged individualism and self-reliance of many Texas cattlemen, who often had to take the law into their own hands. Hittson, however, was not a Texas native. He was born in Nashville, Tennessee, on October 11, 1831. In 1847, when he was sixteen years old, he moved with his parents, Jesse and Polly, to Rusk County between the Sabine and Angelina Rivers in the

Piney Woods of East Texas. That was less than two years after Texas had joined the Union. By 1851, John Hittson had married Selena Frances Brown, and in time, that union would produce ten children. During the early 1850s, times were tough in East Texas. The Hittson family found it difficult to make a living.

In 1855, William Hittson, John's older brother, left home and moved to what is now Palo Pinto County in North Texas. The following year, when the county was established by the Texas state legislature, John Hittson and his family moved there. The brothers slowly began to build their own herds in an area that already had a rich history of cattle ranching. Original settlers in Palo Pinto County included pioneer cattlemen Charles Goodnight, a native of Illinois, who went on to establish the first ranch in the Texas Panhandle, and Oliver Loving, a native of Kentucky, who drove longhorns north to Illinois before the Civil War and later to Denver and New Mexico.

When Palo Pinto County was formally organized in 1857, John Hittson became the first sheriff and served in that office until 1861. As sheriff, he continued ranching, and by 1860, he owned five hundred head of longhorns, but the Civil War brought much change. The Hittson brothers did not join the Confederacy for fear their families would not survive on the Texas frontier. They moved west to Throckmorton County, Texas, and took over Camp Cooper, the abandoned federal military post located on the Clear Fork of the Brazos River. There they remained until about 1866, when they moved their ranching operations to what is now Callahan County on the Staked Plains of West Texas. There they let their cattle roam over a wide area of open range equal to the size of eight counties there today. There was, however, an almost constant threat of Comanche Indians, who roamed the region.

Beginning in 1866, John Hittson annually drove about eight thousand longhorns into New Mexico and north into Colorado, where he sold them. The trail he followed had been laid out in 1865 by James Patterson, a New Mexico beef contractor at Fort Sumner. The trail went up the Middle Concho River valley and then across the plains and up the Pecos River. That route later became known as the Goodnight-Loving Trail after Texas cattlemen Charles Goodnight and Oliver Loving drove a herd of longhorns to Fort Sumner in 1866 and sold them to the military to feed several thousand Indians. Then came

1872, when he raised a small army of cowboys to recover stolen Texas cattle in New Mexico. Politicians in New Mexico protested, but by then, Hittson was in Colorado, where he had an extensive cattle ranching operation near Denver. There is no question that Hittson's invasion slowed cattle stealing by Comanches and their trading with Comancheros, but such trade did not end until the middle 1870s. The U.S. Army finally stopped it after defeating the Comanches and Kiowas on the high plains and sending the surviving remnants to reservations in Indian Territory, now Oklahoma.

As for John Hittson, he moved to Denver, but the panic of 1873 caused some financial reverses. He had to sell many of his cattle to maintain a lavish lifestyle in Denver. Then, too, he had problems with alcohol. When he died in Colorado in 1880, much of his cattle empire was gone.

5

How Cowboys Came to Sing

Some people believe that the singing cowboy was born in Hollywood Westerns during the 1930s to add entertainment to the action films. The truth is that cowboys were singing long before Hollywood introduced singing cowboys. Many years ago, Frank King, a Texan who had driven herds of longhorns up the trails to Kansas, recalled that if a cowboy did not make noise while moving slowly around a herd of cattle bedding down for the night and his horse happened to step against a sleeping steer, the startled steer might jump up, frighten other cattle, and cause a stampede. But if the cowboy rode around the herd singing or whistling in a low voice, said King, the cowboy woke up the cattle nearest to him in a lazy sort of way, and they went back to sleep as the cowboy passed by.

This is how the singing cowboy was born on the open range of Texas during the middle of the nineteenth century. It is doubtful, however, that any of the early singing cowboys could have won a prize for their musical talent. In fact, one old-time cowboy once observed, "Many of the cowboys I knew couldn't carry a tune less'n they pack it over their shoulders in a gunnysack. They'd just say it or speak it off." The early Texas cowboys had two ways of speaking it off. One was loud and vigorous, a way of speaking to prod the slower-moving cattle on the trail. The other way was soft—something like a lullaby—to keep the cattle quiet after they were bedded down for the

23

night. Both ways and types of speaking appear to have started as yelling or talking to cattle. Gradually this gave way to singing. This is only natural because many cowboys had a good sense of rhythm—a rhythm often set by the gait of their horses.

When searching for the origins of cowboy songs early in the twentieth century, folklorist John Lomax remembered when herds of cattle were bedded down a few hundred yards from his boyhood home in Texas. Lomax recalled that on rainy nights, he would hear the cowboys softly singing and calling to the cattle to keep them quiet. When he later described the singing as yodeling, a cattleman told Lomax he was wrong. Lomax then repeated the sounds of what he had heard, and the old cattleman said, "Is that what you call a yodel? We call it humming."

Andy Adams, a cowboy who wrote *The Log of a Cowboy; a Narrative of the Old Trail Days* (1903), once described real cowboy music as a "hybrid between the weirdness of an Indian cry and the croon of a darky mammy."

Regardless of what cowboy singing was called during the nineteenth century, the ability to sing to cattle became an important skill for cowboys when thousands of Texas longhorns were driven to market after the Civil War. Some trail bosses refused to hire a cowboy unless he could sing. Those who could sing often helped to pass the time by thinking up new verses to songs as they drove the longhorns to markets along the Texas coast or to Louisiana or later to the railhead markets in the north.

Texas cattleman J. M. Grigsby recalled that his cowboys "would consider it a dull days drive" if they did not add at least one verse to a song. On dark nights, he said, they looked with high regard on the cowboy who could keep up the most racket singing. Such a cowboy was often called the "bellwether."

Singing to cattle also kept a cowboy awake. The late Montana cowboy and artist, Charlie Russell, once wrote, "The confidence a steer's got in the dark is mighty frail." In threatening weather on a dark night, a ballad or a hymn might quiet the cattle.

On the early Texas trail drives, the cowboys often sang songs they had learned back home, like "Green Grow the Lilacs" and "When You and I Were Young, Maggie," and hymns, especially Methodist ones, plus a few old-fashioned black minstrel songs. By

John Avery Lomax (1867–1948)
grew up in Texas. He spent much
of his life collecting cowboy and
other folk songs. (Courtesy Texas
Folklore Society)

1870, authentic cowboy songs were created as Texans drove thousands upon thousands of longhorns to the railhead towns in Kansas and western Nebraska. The songs that developed on the western plains and prairies between 1870 and about 1900 were simple, and their words reflected the human condition of life on the frontier. They revealed the changing character of the West, especially the shifting frontier, where laws and eastern institutions and traditions were either not effective or nonexistent.

By 1900, however, as more and more eastern ways were established in cattle country, the character of cowboy songs gradually changed. The period of authentic cowboy songs appears to have started during the late 1860s and ended during the 1920s. By 1930, the late nineteenth-century image of a cowboy singing to cattle on trail drives, or to a herd of cattle bedded down for the night, was becoming the model for the singing cowboy on radio and later in motion pictures, where attractive women were substituted for cattle, and the Hollywood cowboy often played the guitar from atop his cow pony.

The real singing cowboy never accompanied himself on a guitar while atop his horse. In fact, the evidence suggests that few cowboys, if they even owned and played Spanish guitars, took their instruments on trail drives. But there are accounts of cowboys carrying and playing fiddles and occasionally a mouth organ. The fiddles were usually carried in the chuck wagon and were played in the evening around the campfire.

There is one account describing a cowboy who sometimes played his fiddle on night guard. It apparently had the same soothing effect on cattle as singing or whistling. But one night an old steer was attracted to the music, and the animal followed the fiddler around the herd until the cowboy stopped playing.

The songs trail driving cowboys sang were not romantic love songs, as Western movies and recordings by some radio entertainers of the 1930s suggested. The authentic cowboy songs reflected their work, their likes and dislikes, their experience and their dreams. They were free from self-consciousness and reflected a sense of what was real and appropriate in their lives.

Although some cowboy songs were adaptations of popular eastern songs of the 1870s and '80s, others were reworked sailor and lumberjack songs. Still others have been traced back to traditional ballads from England, Scotland, and Ireland. Some songs, however, were created by cowboys who borrowed freely from other sources. Such original songs arose out of the rigors and needs of the cowboy on the trail or in a cow camp. It seems likely that the melodies often came before the words were written. Melodies passed along from one cowboy to another eventually were given words by cowboys who were able to capture the mood and the idiom of their work and lives.

Nearly all of the old and really authentic cowboy songs were slow and had something of a pacifying quality. They were, as the late J. Frank Dobie wrote, "as slow as a horse walks around sleeping cattle at night, and the majority of them were mournful." Such songs included night herding songs sung much like a lullaby. One example is a waltz and what many authorities believe is one of the last genuine cowboy songs—"Doney Gal." The words begin:

> We're alone, Doney gal, in the rain and hail,
> Drivin' them doggies on down the trail.

Chorus
It's rain or shine, sleet or snow,
Me an' my Doney gal are on the go,
It's rain or shine, sleet or snow,
Me an' my Doney gal are bound to go.

Most night herding songs convey ideas ranging from mournful to bittersweet. One such song—"Old Paint," sometimes called "I'm A-Leavin' Cheyenne"—was often the last song played at cowboy dances. It was to the cowboy what "Home, Sweet Home" or "Goodnight Ladies" was to people in other walks of life during the twentieth century. The words to one version begin with:

Goodbye, Old Paint, I'm a-leavin' Cheyenne,
Goodbye, Old Paint, I'm a-leavin' Cheyenne,—
My foot in the stirrup, my pony won't stand,
Goodbye, Old Paint, I'm a leavin' Cheyenne.

The words to another version begin with:

I'm a ridin' Old Paint and I'm a leadin' Old Fan,
My foot's in my stirrup, my bridle's in my hand.
Chorus
Goodbye, my little doney, I'm a-leavin' Cheyenne,
Cheyenne-a, Cheyenne, I'm a-leavin' Cheyenne.

Another popular night herding song was actually reshaped from Stephen Foster's old minstrel song titled "Old Uncle Ned." The song is simple; anyone can add a stanza or two if he can make a simple couplet and perceive the lines' rhythms. As a cowboy song, it is titled "The Old Chisholm Trail," and one version begins with:

Oh, I ride with my slicker and I ride all day,
And I pack along a bottle for to pass the time away,
With my feet in the stirrups and my hand on the horn,
I'm the best-damned cowboy that ever was born.
Chorus
Come-a ki-yi-yippee, a bi-yi-yippee, a ki-yi yippee,
    yippee-yay.

The early cowboy songs reflect the melting pot aspects of America. For instance, in tracing the origin of the popular song "Red River Valley," one learns that it was adapted from an upstate New York song titled "The Bright Mohawk Valley," which was carried by British troops into the Red River Valley of the North to put down the Metis rebellion of the late 1860s. The song was carried south and picked up by Texas cowboys who had driven cattle north. In time, the song became popular and many people assumed the Red River Valley in the title was the Red River between Texas and what is now Oklahoma. Another song, "The Cowboy's Stroll" (sometimes called "Jack O'Diamonds"), did not originate in cattle country but came from an Irish ballad titled "The Forsaken Girl."

What became another popular cowboy song has been traced to Maine in the 1850s, where lumberjacks sang "The Lumberman's Life." It was adapted by someone in the West, perhaps James Barton Adams, and was called "Cowboy's Life Is a Dreary, Dreary Life." Another version was simply titled "A Cowboy's Life." The words to one version begin with:

> A cowboy's life is a weary, dreary life,
> Some say it's free from care,
> Round up the cattle from morning til night,
> In the middle of the prairie so bare.

The song "The Gal I Left Behind Me" was once thought to have originated with cowboys, but it has since been traced back to the eighteenth century. Early in the nineteenth century, it was popular in eastern music halls before it found its way west to be sung by cowboys.

"The Buffalo Skinners" was often thought to be a cowboy song, but the melody has been traced to a nineteenth-century English song reworked by lumberjacks in Canada. Eventually it was reworked again to tell the true story of some cowboys who were hired at Jacksboro in North Texas to go out on the plains beyond the Pease River to skin buffaloes.

The words to "The Cowboy's Dream" are original to cattle country, but the melody is that of the well-known air, "My Bonnie Lies Over the Ocean." The words created by cowboys begin with:

> Last night as I lay on the prairie,
> And looked at the stars in the sky,
> I wondered if ever a cowboy
> Would drift to that sweet by and by.

Chorus
Roll on, roll on;
Roll on, little doggies, roll on, roll on,
Roll on, roll on;
Roll on, little doggies, roll on.

The popular cowboy song "Little Joe, the Wrangler" was written by
N. Howard "Jack" Thorp in 1898 in West Texas or eastern New
Mexico. It is a sentimental piece, which Thorp said was woven around
an actual event on the trail. It was first sung to the air of "Little Old
Log Cabin in the Lane" and has the perennial theme of the under-
dog. Its words begin with:

> Little Joe, the wrangler, will never wrangle more,
> His days with the Remuda—they are done.
> T'was a year ago last April he joined the outfit here,
> A little Texas Stray and all alone.

Teddy Blue, an early cowboy on the northern plains, remembered a
song called "Cowboy Annie," a woman with questionable morals
who liked cowboys. The song begins with these words:

> Cowboy Annie was her name,
> And the Bar N outfit was her fame,
> And when the beef is four year old,
> We'll fill her pillowslips with gold.

What many people consider a cowboy classic, the melody of
"Bury Me Not on the Lone Prairie"—sometimes called "The Dying
Cowboy"—was actually borrowed from the sentimental parlor ballad
titled "The Ocean Burial," written during the 1870s. The words:

> O bury me not on the lone prairie,
> These words came low and mournfully,
> From the pallid lips of a youth who lay,
> On his dying bed at the close of the day.
> *Chorus*
> O bury me not on the lone prairie,
> When the wild cayotes will howl o'er me,
> In a narrow grave just six by three,
> O bury me not on the lone prairie.

The theme of a dying cowboy is commonplace in many cowboy songs, and the semantics still cause confusion. "The Cowboy's Lament," supposedly a variant on a verse titled "The Dying Girl's Lament," is sometimes called "The Dying Cowboy." However, it began as an Irish ballad and apparently was adapted to the American cowboy by Francis Henry "Frank" Maynard, born in 1853. He spent a decade as a cowboy and set his version at the door of Tom Sherman's bar in Dodge City, Kansas. Texas cowboys at Wichita in 1876 learned the song and transferred the locale to Laredo, Texas. The song became known as "The Streets of Laredo." It tells the sad story of a cowpuncher shot in a gambling brawl. It is one song that comes about as close as any other single song to supplying all of the elements of an epic of the American West. It deals with the death of a sinner, remorse, and death, three elements of deep concern to most cowboys. In the song, a cowboy, dying in a street or on a barroom floor, tries to capture the ear of a fellow cowboy to purge his soul for the last ride. The words to the most popular version begin with:

> As I walked out in the streets of Laredo,
> As I walked out in Laredo one day,
> I spied a poor cowboy wrapped up in white linen,
> Wrapped up in white linen as cold as the clay.
> *Chorus*
> Oh, beat the drum slowly and play the fife lowly,
> Play the Dead March as you carry me along,
> Take me to the green valley, there lay the sod o'er me,
> For I'm a young cowboy and I know I've done wrong.

In looking back, the melodies of cowboy songs during the late nineteenth century were not set in stone. Rarely did cowboys sing together. Generally, each cowboy had a different kind of tune that he would sing—one or more favorites. A favorite of cowboys on the trail was "Morning Grub Holler," sometimes called "Cowboy's Getting-up Holler." Its words:

> Wake up, Jacob,
> Day's a-breakin',
> Peas in the pot
> And the hoecake's bakin'!
> Early in the morning,
> Almost day,

If you don't come soon,
Gonna throw it all away
Wake up, Jacob!
Bacon in the pan,
Coffee in the pot,
Get up and get it—
Get it while it's hot,
Wake, snakes, and bite a biscuit!

"Home on the Range" is often considered a cowboy song, but in reality, it is a granger's, or homesteader's, song. "Home on the Range" really became popular in 1933, when a group of newspapermen standing outside the home of Franklin D. Roosevelt in New York City sang the song. That day, the American people had elected Roosevelt president.

When Roosevelt heard them singing it, he came outside and asked them to sing it again. They did, and Roosevelt supposedly said, "That's my favorite song." Overnight, "Home on the Range" became popular. By 1934, just about every radio station in America was

Dr. Brewster Higley wrote the words to "Home on the Range." (Courtesy Kansas State Historical Society)

Daniel E. Kelley wrote the music
to "Home on the Range."
(Courtesy Kansas State Historical
Society)

playing the song on the air. Record companies, music publishers—everyone connected with the music business—were taking advantage of "Home on the Range" because there were no royalties to pay. The song was not copyrighted. The author or authors were unknown. The song's mood fit the dreams of Americans caught in the Great Depression of the 1930s.

It was then that an Arizona couple claimed they had written "Home on the Range" under the title "An Arizona Home." They went to court and sought half a million dollars in damages because they had copyrighted their song in 1905. Quickly music publishers pulled "Home on the Range" sheet music off music store shelves; recording companies stopped selling records of the song. Radio stations were warned not to play the tune on the air.

The Music Publishers Protective Association took over the defense of the suit, and their attorney, Samuel Moanfeldt, spent three months tracking down the origin of the song. He found the words had been written about 1873 in Smith County, Kansas, under the title "My Western Home." The author was a medical doctor, Dr. Brewster Higley, who wrote the words in his one-room dugout home on Beaver

Roy Rogers (1912–1998) starred as a singing cowboy in nearly ninety westerns for Republic pictures. He is shown with his wife and costar Dale Evans. (Author's Collection)

Creek near modern Smith Center. Moanfeldt learned that Higley had died in Oklahoma in 1909. Moanfeldt also learned the music to "Home on the Range" was written by Daniel E. Kelley, a native of Rhode Island, who settled in Kansas in 1872. Kelley died in Iowa in 1905.

With this evidence, Moanfeldt and the Music Publishers Protective Association won the case, and the song has been played freely ever since. On the basis of the evidence Moanfeldt discovered, the Kansas legislature made "Home on the Range" the official state song of Kansas in 1947, and it remains a popular song beyond that state's borders today.

Folklorists and collectors of cowboy songs are the first to admit that the more they look into cowboy songs, the more they realize how many variants there are—not only in melodies but in words. Since the middle nineteenth century, cowboy songs have evolved. Hollywood made the singing cowboy known to every household, with Western stars like Gene Autry and Roy Rogers. Cowboy music continues to evolve and remains popular.

Gene Autry (1907–1998) starred in more than ninety Westerns for Republic and Columbia pictures as a singing cowboy. Here he is shown next to his horse Champion. (Author's Collection)

For some people, such songs offer escape from modern life. For others, they provide simple pleasure and enjoyment. The slow cowboy songs are peaceful and relaxing, and they hark back to days when life was simpler. When compared to all other types of folk songs, cowboy songs are probably more typical of America than any other aspect of our folk-song heritage. For that reason alone, they should be preserved for future generations.

6

A Trail Drive Honeymoon

For Texans driving herds of longhorns north to markets in Kansas, the year 1877 was different than previous years. It was Dodge City's first year as a cattle town, thanks in part to the arrival of the Atchison, Topeka, and Santa Fe Railroad. It also was the year that D. Wilborn "Doc" Barton, age twenty-seven, drove his second herd of longhorns north to Kansas from central Texas. His herd was one of many that trailed north that year, but Barton's trail drive was different from the rest. Although he had a similar complement of men and equipment as that found with the other drives—eight cowboys plus a black cook, a string of horses, and a chuck wagon—he apparently was the only trail driver making the journey with his wife and baby, and it was their honeymoon.

The Bartons' story began five years earlier, in 1872, when D. W. Barton, then twenty, and his older brother, Alfred Hightower Barton, twenty-five, decided to drive a herd of longhorns to market in Kansas. Two of their friends, J. D. "Dee" Eubank and Tom Connell, who would later became cattlemen in their own right, joined the Barton brothers on the journey. They left the Barton family ranch in Mason County, Texas, near present-day Round Rock north of Austin, with a herd of three thousand longhorns in February.

In 1872, D. W. Barton was not yet called "Doc." That came later, but how he got the nickname is still something of a mystery.

One account says an uncle who was a medical doctor gave him the name. Another says his first name was really "Doctor," and still another says cowboys gave him the nickname after he helped deliver his wife's second baby. The last account might be true. We do know that for Doc Barton, a long trail drive was a new experience, as it was for his friends, Dee Eubank and Tom Connell, but Doc's older brother, Al Barton, had much experience on the trail. A few years earlier, he had hired out to help drive two thousand five hundred cattle to California. As they began driving their herd north, everyone asked Al Barton for advice.

The Barton brothers started north, intending to cross Indian Territory into Kansas, but they soon learned that there were Indian raids in north Texas. The Barton brothers had heard about such raids from their father Decater (sometimes spelled Decator) Barton, who had been wounded seven times by Indian arrows in raids in Texas. The brothers decided to avoid such problems with hostile Indians in north Texas. They turned their herd northwest and followed the Pecos River into New Mexico. There they turned north, skirting the Sangre de Cristo Mountains, and traveled through Trinchera Pass into Colorado to avoid "Uncle Dick" Wootton's toll road over Raton Pass, which had been completed five years earlier. At Pueblo, Colorado, the Barton brothers followed the Arkansas River east, past the site of modern Rocky Ford.

As they pushed east into unsettled country, they saw buffalo still roaming the plains, along with packs of gray wolves following the herds looking for an easy meal. As the trail drive crossed into what is now southwest Kansas, D. W. Barton became enthusiastic about the country. Along the Arkansas River was tallgrass in the bottoms, rich shortgrass on the uplands, and plenty of water. Because the land had fed buffalo for decades, Barton knew it was ideal grazing country for cattle. The Barton brothers decided to fatten their cattle on the rich grasses of southwest Kansas before selling them. Their cattle would be more valuable. The brothers set up a camp by Lone Tree, the remains of an immense cottonwood near the site of modern-day Garden City, Kansas. The tree's giant trunk had been half burned and almost stripped of branches to furnish fuel for travelers following the Santa Fe Trail, but its trunk served as their camp marker and the spot where open range cattle ranching began in southwest Kansas.

With the winter of 1872 approaching, the Barton brothers made their camp several miles southeast down the Arkansas River, near present-day Pierceville, Kansas, and built a dugout on a high bank above the Arkansas River. They hoped it would keep them warm in the winter cold. The cattle with the OS brand ranged as far as Cimarron, about twenty miles to the east and south beyond the Cimarron River in what is now the Oklahoma Panhandle.

Although the Santa Fe Trail had long crossed this region, the countless freight wagons of earlier years had dwindled in number because of the arrival of the railroad. The only nearby settlement was Fort Dodge, about forty-five miles east of the Barton's winter camp. Established in 1865 between two fordable crossings of the Arkansas River, the post at first was nothing more than a collection of sod dugouts, ten by twelve feet in circumference and seven feet deep. What later became the town of Dodge City located just west of the fort, which then consisted of one run-down shack.

D. W. Barton loved the country. The grass fattened the cattle. Many of their animals were then driven east to Great Bend, Kansas, and sold. The next spring, Doc Barton left his older brother and two friends, who made up what they called the Barton Cattle Company, to watch the unsold cattle and returned to Texas to gather another herd. Another reason for returning to Texas was that Doc Barton missed the girl he had left behind. When he returned to Mason County, Texas, Doc apparently spent more time with his girl, Belle Vandeveer, than in gathering another cattle herd. Belle was the daughter of Berry Vandeveer, a rancher in nearby Burnet County, Texas.

Soon Belle and D. W. Barton were married. She knew her husband wanted to return to southwest Kansas, but she was less enthusiastic than he was about moving to Kansas. Her parents, along with four brothers and three sisters, lived in Texas. But her husband's enthusiasm for southwest Kansas was apparently catching. Within a few months, Belle agreed to leave Texas. Doc Barton started to gather a herd of longhorns and make plans to drive them to Kansas, but there was another delay. Belle gave birth to a baby girl. Doc was an excited father, but in the spring of 1877, he was ready to leave with the cattle for southwest Kansas. He suggested to his wife that she and the baby travel by train to Kansas City and then west to Dodge City on the newly completed Santa Fe line. Belle Barton, however, said she would have none of it and firmly told her husband, "Whither thou goest, I will go." She had lived her life on her father's Texas ranch. She could ride well, and she knew all of the techniques used in rounding up and driving cattle. The prospects of a trail drive did not frighten her. Doc Barton, a tall man with blue eyes that always seemed to twinkle, realized his wife had a strong will. He did not argue with her but made plans for the drive.

With nine cowboys, a black cook called Uncle Ed, a string of good horses, and a chuck wagon, Barton, his wife, and their baby daughter set out from Mason County in central Texas for Kansas with a herd of three thousand longhorns, including five hundred head that Belle's father had given the couple as a wedding present. When not riding horseback, she left the baby in the care of Uncle Ed in the chuck wagon. When Belle Barton drove the wagon, Doc watched the baby.

How much of a honeymoon it was is not known. The drive north was mostly uneventful. No Indian problems were reported in North Texas, so he decided to cross Indian Territory into Kansas. There were no stampedes on the journey. There were no Indian attacks, but on two different occasions, they did encounter Indians as they crossed Indian Territory. The first time, Barton spotted a band of Indians approaching the herd from some distance. They did not appear to be hostile. Barton told his wife and cowboys, "Stand still and look them straight in the eyes. Do not draw a gun unless I give the order." The Indians raced toward the herd, then stopped within a few feet of where Barton and his wife were standing near the chuck wagon. Barton made them a sign of friendship. The Indians responded accordingly and inspected the wagon. When they found the Barton baby, the Indians were delighted and tried to attract its attention. When they tired of the play, the Indians got back on their ponies and rode away.

The second time they encountered Indians was while Mrs. Barton was driving the chuck wagon. Another party of Indians approached and headed for the chuck wagon, which was perhaps a quarter mile beyond the herd. As the Indians raced toward the wagon, Mrs. Barton hid the baby and tried to catch up with the herd. The Indians, however, frightened the horses that were pulling the chuck wagon, and it became stuck in a rut as the Indians reached it. To Belle Barton's surprise, the Indians leaped off their ponies and lifted the wagon out of the rut. As her husband rode up to the wagon, his wife was thanking the Indians for their help and emptying a two-gallon jar of cookies into their hands. When the cookies were gone, the Indians, laughing, got back on their ponies and rode away.

Soon after reaching the Barton camp, which was near the site of modern Pierceville, Kansas, they learned of Indian raids in the area. At Al Barton's suggestion, the brothers moved their cattle to Crooked Creek near the present-day town of Meade, Kansas, near what is now the Oklahoma Panhandle. Once the Bartons got settled in a dugout along Wolf Creek, Al Barton said it was his turn to go back to Texas and get another herd of longhorns. He missed his girlfriend, Mollie Moreland, in Burnet County, Texas. When he reached Texas, Al Barton lost no time in proposing to Mollie, and they were married. From all indications, she accompanied her husband on the trail drive north, just as Belle Barton had done. Whether or not they considered the drive their honeymoon is not known. Al Barton delivered the herd to his younger brother and family, who had in the meantime moved to an abandoned stockade with a small house and cellar on Wolf Creek. The stockade had been built a few years earlier by Charles "Dirty Face" Jones and Joseph Plummer, two former buffalo hunters who tried unsuccessfully to operate a trading post at the stockade.

After Indian hostilities ended in southwest Kansas by 1881, Barton sold the stockade and twelve hundred cattle to Texas rancher Henry W. Cresswell for eighteen dollars a head. Doc Barton, Belle, and their children—five boys and two girls—returned to Kansas and settled near what is now the town of Cimarron, as did his brother, Al, and his wife. The brothers built homes for their families and began to make good money from cattle and land investments. In 1882, D. W. Barton traveled south through Texas to Louisiana, where he purchased three thousand cattle and hired some cowboys to drive the animals to southwest Kansas.

The Barton brothers and their families enjoyed pleasant lives near Cimarron, Kansas, until January 1886, when a winter blizzard with very cold temperatures swept across the plains south from Canada. Remembered as "the terrible blizzard of 1886," the vicious weather contributed to the collapse of many cattle empires, including that of the Barton brothers. Their herd of twelve thousand, plus eight hundred registered cattle, drifted with the storm and scattered, bunching in draws and canyons near the Cimarron River and against barbed-wire fences. When the Barton brothers went looking for their cattle after the storm, they found eleven thousand cattle frozen to death. Doc and Al Barton found themselves out of the cattle business. Al Barton's wife soon died, and he returned to Texas, where in 1890 he married a woman, also named Mollie, and became a rancher in Motley County near Lubbock until his death in 1921.

As for Doc Barton, after the blizzard of 1886, he remained in what is now Gray County, Kansas, which had been organized in 1881. He and his family were the first settlers. After the town of Ingalls was established in 1884, the family lived there. Doc Barton raised a few head of cattle but began concentrating on wheat ranching, as he called it, and in land investments. Doc Barton never filed on a homestead but instead bought cheap land, figuring it cost him less money to buy than to prove up on a government homestead. For a time, Doc Barton served as sheriff of Gray County and was one of the oldest pioneers in southwest Kansas until his death in Dodge City on January 12, 1946, at the age of ninety-five. From what is known, his wife died seventeen years before, in 1929, fifty-two years after their honeymoon on the trail drive to Kansas.

7

When Billy Carried the News

It was just before midnight on January 29, 1861. The foreman in the back shop of a Missouri newspaper was waiting for printers to hand-set the last type so that he could lock the material in the forms. Lounging nearby was the pressman waiting to lock the forms on the press to print the morning edition of the *St. Joseph Daily Gazette.*

One of the compositors setting type—I shall call him Billy because his real name has been lost in time—was young, a recent arrival in St. Joseph. Billy was something of a tramp printer who found it difficult to settle down in any one town. He seemed to migrate with the seasons, going west in the spring when the birds began to sing but returning east to Missouri about the time of the first frost to find winter work at any newspaper that would hire him.

On one of his western trips, he made friends with Thomas White, a prominent farmer and stock raiser, who lived on the rolling grasslands of the Flint Hills near Council Grove in Kansas Territory. In 1859, White was appointed a justice of the peace. White and young Billy became friends.

When Billy returned to Missouri in the fall of 1860 and found a job with the St. Joseph paper, he wrote White, telling him where he was working. He said he was pleased with the newspaper because it received news by telegraph from the east. At the time, no newspaper in Kansas Territory to the west had telegraph service.

In his reply, White asked Billy to watch for news that Kansas had been admitted to the Union. When the news came, White asked Billy to get word to him at the earliest possible moment, regardless of the expense.

Nearly everyone in Kansas knew that about three months earlier, the House of Representatives had passed a bill to admit Kansas to the Union as a free state, but the Senate, controlled by proslavery elements, rejected it. Kansans apparently believed that statehood was not possible in the foreseeable future. Three weeks later, however, Abraham Lincoln was elected president, and a bit later, Jefferson Davis and other southern senators withdrew from the Senate, giving that body a free state majority.

It was then that the bill to admit Kansas to the Union was reintroduced and passed on January 21, several weeks before Lincoln was inaugurated. Because of a Senate amendment concerning the judiciary, the bill had to go back to the House of Representatives. The bill was finally passed on January 28.

As Billy was setting type that evening, the last news item received by telegraph reported that President James Buchanan had that very day signed the bill in Washington. Kansas was now a state. As soon as the story was set in type and handed to the foreman, he locked it in the form, and the pressman began to print the morning edition.

Billy quickly put his printer's apron on a hook, got his coat, and tendered his resignation to the foreman. He asked one of his printer friends to get his fleet-footed pony that had been groomed and foddered at Kate Bugess's nearby livery stable. When Billy told the foreman he wanted the pay owed to him, he was told that Jule Robidoux, the newspaper's clerk who paid the printers, had already gone home.

When Billy explained to another printer, Oscar Leonard, why he had to leave, Leonard loaned Billy twenty dollars and got in exchange a note asking the clerk to pay Leonard the money due Billy.

It was just past two o'clock on the cold morning of January 30 when Billy, dressed warmly, tucked two or three copies of the freshly printed *St. Joseph Daily Gazette* into one side of his saddlebags. In the other side was a wet lunch—a bottle of brandy—to help him keep warm. Billy mounted his fiery little pony and headed a few blocks west to the frozen Missouri River. Crossing on the ice just below the

"Robidoux brick," a brick row house built in 1843, Billy's pony climbed the steep bank, taking Billy into the new state of Kansas.

Heading southwest, Billy's pony made good time. It was a cold and clear night. The stars twinkled brightly as the pony carried Billy deeper into the new state. A few hours later, as the first rays of light appeared on the eastern horizon, Billy reached Independence Creek. Smoke was curling skyward from a settler's cabin as Billy reined his pony to a stop. The settler invited Billy inside and gave him some breakfast and hot coffee.

Billy stayed long enough to eat and warm himself in front of the fire, and to tell the settler that Kansas was now a state. Thanking the settler for his hospitality, Billy climbed atop his pony and continued southwest. He did not stop until he rode through Topeka at about two o'clock in the afternoon. Outside of Topeka, he stopped at the cabin of Jo Jim, a half-breed Kansa Indian, whose real name was Joseph James, the son of a white man and Indian woman.

James had lived in the area for more than twenty-five years, had served as an Indian interpreter, and had become a prominent farmer and stockman. There James gave Billy another hot meal and another pony. Climbing atop his new mount, Billy headed southwest toward Council Grove.

The sun had already set when Billy reached Mission Creek, where he stopped at a settler's cabin and took supper. It was just past midnight when Billy reined his tired mount at the farm of Thomas White. Billy knocked on the door. When White opened it, he smiled, realizing it was Billy. The tired rider handed White the copies of the *St. Joseph Daily Gazette* as White ushered Billy into his home. While White's wife prepared a hot meal for Billy, the two men drank to the new state. While Billy ate and relaxed, White read the newspaper before a blazing fire. Before falling asleep, Billy congratulated himself. He had covered one hundred forty miles in about twenty-two hours. He figured he was the first person to travel any distance in the new state of Kansas.

8

When Women Were Scarce

From Kansas northward through the Dakotas, white women were often scarce during the latter half of the nineteenth century. When the Kansas and Nebraska Territories were opened to settlement in 1854, many men left their wives and sweethearts in the east to come west to settle. Once they established their homes, they sent east for their womenfolk or went back and brought them west.

When the Homestead Act became law toward the end of the Civil War, many men followed the same practice. Those fearing that they might lose their land to claim jumpers if they went east simply sent for their wives or sweethearts. Others took their chances and left their claims. One man took the precaution of posting a notice on the door of his homestead house that read, "Back soon.—Gone to get a wife."

The disparity of women to men in early Kansas and Nebraska territories made finding a wife a highly competitive task. Certainly there were some women, but most were married. In 1857, the Kansas Territorial Legislature voted down a bill to license marriages on the grounds that the lawmakers did not wish to place any obstacles in the way of marriage "when the women were so hard to get."

In some areas, women were so scarce that men turned to advertising for them in newspapers. The *Walnut Valley Times* of El Dorado, Kansas, on July 1, 1870, ran the following paid notice:

Wanted—Fifty young ladies to make husbands of fifty, well-to-do bachelors residing in and about El Dorado. While our population is increasing there is yet only half the material here to further comply with the Governor's request, if we only had the other half.

In nearby Wichita one young man was so desperate that he paid to have the following ad published in the *Vidette* on September 9, 1870. It read:

Girls Attention! We are authorized to state that the first good, respectable young lady, who settles in Slate Creek, Sumner County, will receive a present of a fine saddle horse, saddle and bridle, and a husband if she wants one. Here, girls is a chance for you. We will guarantee that the party making the offer will carry out his part of the bargain in good faith, provided the young lady in question accepts the proposition.

How successful the advertisers were is not known, but the search for women continued into the late 1870s. In fact, the *People's Tribune* in Jefferson City, Missouri, May 22, 1872, listed half a dozen men looking for women under the headline, "Take Your Pick, Girls!" Two of the advertisements read:

Mr. R.W.W. is a demi-blonde, tall, talented, and tolerably good looking, dark gray eyes, sandy hair and whiskers, aged about 35 years. Would make an excellent husband, but is very shy and hard to catch.

Mr. J.L.P. is an incorrigible bachelor of several winters, about five feet eight inches in height, hard to catch, is a great admirer of ladies, but does not desire a warranter deed to any particular one. Thoroughly understands the management of a small tea party, and would prove a treasure as a family man. Will not keep longer than 1873.

In time, even a few unattached women sought husbands. One such woman in Dakota Territory sent a letter to a Montana weekly newspaper in 1882: "I mean business. If there is a young man in this country that has as much sand in him as a pound of plug tobacco, I want to hear from him. I have a tree claim, a homestead, am a good cook, am not afraid of work, and am willing to do my part. If any of you young men with a like amount of land, a decent face and carcass, wants a good wife, I can fill the bill," she wrote. Whether or not she got a husband is not recorded.

Then there is the story of a circuit rider in Kansas who became proficient in performing quick marriages. The Ellsworth, Kansas, *Reporter,* January 16, 1872, reported, "Last week we announced the marriage of a young friend, and now it becomes our pleasant duty to announce that he is the father of a bouncing boy."

Another story is set in Meade County, Kansas, in the 1870s. A drifter was found guilty of disorderly conduct. The same day, a woman was found guilty of vagrancy. Both were sentenced to jail and did not have the money to pay their fines. The judge who found them guilty was in a quandary because the jail had no quarters for women. The man and woman talked about the situation and offered to solve the problem by getting married. The judge agreed. A collection was taken up to pay for a marriage license. The judge performed the marriage at no cost, and the newlyweds were escorted to the jail for their honeymoon.

A different sort of situation was reported by the *Prairie Owl,* January 14, 1886, at Fargo Springs, a settlement founded in 1865 about thirteen miles north of Liberal in far southwest Kansas. After the railroad bypassed the town in 1888, everyone left, but two years earlier, it was a growing community. About eight o'clock one evening in 1886, a shy boy and a young country girl walked into the judge's office. They asked to see the judge. The clerk said the judge was gone until morning. The boy and girl were shaken. They wanted the judge to marry them.

The clerk suggested they go to the town's hotel and come back in the morning. The boy explained that they had only fifty cents, just enough for one bed. The clerk thought for a moment and proposed a solution. He told them that as a clerk, he could perform the ceremony, provided they come back in the morning and let the judge do it again. Otherwise, said the clerk, the marriage will not hold up. The couple promised they would come back the next morning. The clerk then performed the ceremony, and the smiling couple then hurried off in the direction of the town's hotel.

By the late nineteenth century, men and women establishing claims had learned a few tricks. Jack Potter, an early cowboy and cattleman, told the story about some young women who took four claims and then built a four-room shack over the four innermost touching corners of their claims. This way they could still live together but could establish residence on their respective claims.

Three of the women were well educated, but the fourth was of husky pioneer stock. A few miles away was a ranch where the cowboys were usually on the alert for new nester neighbors. When the cowboys would pass the house built by the four young women, they never saw a man around. One day, one of the cowpunchers rode into the ranch headquarters. He was excited and informed everyone that there were a bunch of women living in the house—and there were no men.

When asked how he knew this, he replied, "I got my evidence from the clothes line. Not a man's garment was on it. These women are practicing economy, too, as some of their liner-wear has flour marks on it."

For the cowboys, getting friendly with the four women was a slow business. One day, the cowboys saw the husky woman pass the ranch headquarters driving a wagon to get cedar brakes for wood and posts. Some of the cowboys named her Covered Wagon Kate. One of the cowboys was a middle-aged bachelor nicknamed Rant'n Peter. He had always been shy around women. Covered Wagon Kate, however, relaxed to friendly overtures from Rant'n Peter. In a few months, the cowboy and "Kate" were married and within a year had a baby. What happened to the other three women is not known.

Part II

BURIED TREASURE LEGENDS

I had been every kind of fool except one. I had expended my patrimony, pretended my matrimony, played poker, lawn-tennis, and bucket shops—parted soon with my money in many ways. But there remained one role of the wearer of cap and bells that I had not played. That was the Seeker after Buried Treasure.
—O. Henry

Some Words about Treasure Legends

The treasure legends that follow are stories. They are not intended as road maps to follow to discover great wealth. Nearly every human at one time or another has dreamed of suddenly finding great wealth. It is an age-old dream that seems to lie in human nature.

Possibly the wildest wild-goose chase in the recorded history of the American West was Coronado's search for the fabled Quivira, or the Seven Cities of Cibola. The treasure-seeking Spaniards wandered over more than three thousand miles of land previously unexplored by Europeans, much of it on the plains, in search of cities where streets were supposedly paved with gold.

Since then, many legends of lost mines and buried treasure have developed along the routes believed to be taken by Coronado and the other Spanish explorers who followed. Countless other treasure legends exist along many other trails used by other explorers, gold miners, outlaws, settlers, wagon freighters, and traders who later crisscrossed the prairies and plains from Canada to Mexico and from the eastern slopes of the Rocky Mountains east to the Missouri River.

Some of the more interesting buried treasure legends are linked in one manner or another to travelers. Many such legends have some basis in fact, and in a few instances, there is good reason to believe the treasures may still exist, if they weren't already found and quickly removed without fanfare to avoid the tax collector. Other treasure tales, however, are probably little more than wishful thinking on the part of those who passed them down from generation to generation and embellished them along the way to make the story more appealing.

9

The Tres Piedras Legend

This tale begins in about 1800, when Pierre LaFarge, an excommunicated French priest, was released from jail in France after serving time for killing a man. LaFarge sailed for America. Although he had been kicked out of the Catholic church, he posed as a priest to find lodging and food as he traveled across America. In New Orleans, he met a group of twelve other Frenchmen who were shady characters in their own right. LaFarge joined them in sailing across the Gulf of Mexico to Matamoros, Mexico. The former priest fit in perfectly with the other Frenchmen. All of them were determined to fill their pockets with anything valuable in the New World.

In Mexico, they learned that someone had buried silver and gold near Chihuahua for safekeeping. Ten heavily armed Mexicans guarded the treasure. Deciding to steal only the gold, the fully armed Frenchmen surprised the Mexican guards and killed all but two. LaFarge and the other Frenchmen carried off more than one hundred pounds of the gold, but left the less valuable silver. Meanwhile, the surviving guards notified Spanish authorities, who went after the robbers. LaFarge and the others fled north with the gold into what is now New Mexico.

When they reached the sleepy village of Santa Fe, they learned that gold had been discovered in the mountains somewhere near

Taos, to the north. They traveled there and soon set up a mining operation near several small streams. Not having much mining experience, they found only a little gold, but posing as miners was the perfect cover for disposing of some of the stolen Mexican gold.

In time, they learned that more experienced Mexican miners working nearby had much better success finding gold. Many months after LaFarge and the Frenchmen arrived near Taos, they decided the nearby Mexican miners had accumulated sufficient gold worth stealing.

As the story is told, LaFarge and the others began robbing and killing more than twenty Mexican miners in the region around Taos. After a few months, the Frenchmen acquired much gold, but their robbing had been costly. The Mexican miners did not give up their gold easily. Six of the Frenchmen were killed in the robberies, leaving only LaFarge and six Frenchmen.

Somewhere in the mountains near Taos, the seven men discussed what to do with all of the gold they had accumulated. LaFarge believed it should be taken back to France, where all of them could enjoy life to its fullest. The others agreed. The men decided that LaFarge should pose as a priest, go to Santa Fe, find someone with smelting experience, and bring that person back to turn the gold into ingots.

Sometime during the summer of 1804, LaFarge found José Lopat, a native of Spain, about thirty-five years old, living in Santa Fe. Lopat had worked with metals in Mexico City before moving north to Santa Fe. He returned with LaFarge to the mountains near Taos, where Lopat built a small furnace and constructed a mold. It took him three months to convert the gold into seven hundred ingots, each weighing seven and a quarter pounds. Together, all the gold ingots weighed more than five thousand pounds.

Their plan was to take the gold to New Orleans, where they thought they could easily ship it to France. To prepare for the journey, LaFarge and the six other Frenchmen acquired oxen and six large oxcarts, which they filled with fur pelts. Outwardly, the carts appeared to be filled with furs, but hidden underneath were the gold ingots, which were divided equally among the ox carts. The Frenchmen then hired about fifteen Indian servants, obtained supplies, and started east from the mountains onto the plains of what is now northeastern

New Mexico. José Lopat traveled with them because he said he knew the country.

Exactly what happened next is not clear, but the party apparently followed trails used by Spaniards, Mexicans, Indians, and other travelers. They traveled east into what is now the Oklahoma Panhandle. Part of the trail may have been what later was called the dry route of the Santa Fe Trail. Although the journey was slow because of the weight carried in the oxcarts, it apparently was uneventful until they reached a watering hole called Flag Springs near the modern town of Boise City, Oklahoma, and several miles east of Black Mesa, the highest point in Oklahoma at just under five thousand feet, in Cimarron County, Oklahoma. The county is the only one in the United States that borders four states—Colorado, Kansas, New Mexico, and Texas. At Flag Springs, the party found four traders who were heading west. One of the Frenchmen supposedly mentioned to the traders that they were taking furs to New Orleans because they believed they could get a better price from fellow Frenchmen than the Spanish in New Spain, who resented the French. The Frenchmen were surprised when they learned from the traders that France had sold Louisiana Territory to the United States in 1803.

LaFarge and the four Frenchmen did not outwardly show much concern about the news until the four traders broke camp and continued west. The Frenchmen then had a serious discussion and concluded that when they reached New Orleans, the American authorities probably would not permit them to ship their gold to France; they would likely confiscate it. When José Lopat was asked his opinion, he said maybe arrangements could be made for a boat to meet the party along the Gulf Coast to transport the gold. He suggested that two of the best-fit Frenchmen travel ahead to New Orleans to see what kind of arrangements could be made, and then return. Lopat said such a round trip would probably take three and a half months. LaFarge and the four Frenchmen decided to take Lopat's advice.

Two of the Frenchmen set out for New Orleans while LaFarge and the other two Frenchmen made a temporary camp near Flag Springs. When four months had passed and the two Frenchmen had not returned from New Orleans, LaFarge and the remaining Frenchmen decided to bury the gold for safety. They also agreed that it would be a good idea to send José Lopat and the Indian servants back to Santa Fe before they buried the gold. To make certain they would leave and not stop and come back to watch where the Frenchmen buried the gold, at least one of the Frenchmen escorted Lopat and the Indians more than a hundred miles in the direction of Santa Fe. Details on what happened next are hazy, but the gold was buried in the ground near Flag Springs, and apparently stone markers were buried nearby in the ground.

About a year passed. LaFarge, whose health was failing, returned to Santa Fe, where José Lopat happened to see him on the street. LaFarge told Lopat that all of the Frenchmen were dead and that he alone knew where the gold was buried near the spring. LaFarge apparently claimed that Indians had killed the others, but Lopat suspected LaFarge had killed the remaining Frenchmen. Regardless, Lopat learned LaFarge was suffering from tuberculosis. He had returned to Santa Fe in hopes that the higher altitude would cure him. Once it did, he planned to return to Flag Springs and recover the gold ingots.

LaFarge never returned. His health got worse. Soon he was bedridden. Next a relative of a miner killed by LaFarge learned that LaFarge was in Santa Fe. The relative organized a posse to lynch LaFarge, but the former priest learned this, and with the help of a friend, LaFarge was placed in an oxcart under hay and taken somewhere outside of Santa Fe, where he died two weeks later.

After learning of LaFarge's death, José Lopat decided to journey to Flag Springs and locate the buried gold, but after searching, he found nothing, not even any signs of digging. He soon returned to Santa Fe, where he later died on June 4, 1856, at the age of about eighty-seven years.

If it had not been for Lopat, however, the legend of the buried gold might have faded into history. Lopat's son, Emanuel, born in 1819, heard the story many times from his father and wrote it down in Spanish in the back of the Lopat family Bible. After Emanuel died in Denver, Colorado, in 1906, his sister, Angelina, gained possession of it. After she died in 1925, the Bible was inherited by her niece, Mrs. Frank Boyles, of Denver.

Efforts to locate the Lopat family Bible today have not been successful, but it contains more than fifty pages that tell José Lopat's story

written down by his son Emanuel. It is the basis for the legend. Before
he died in 1856, the old man began to tell the story, knowing he
would never be able to return to Flag Springs. Since the early 1840s,
the legend has spread by word of mouth across the plains. Many treasure seekers have tried to find the gold, but no one has ever admitted
to success. Today the ingots would be worth at least $2 million.

10

Treasure Tales from the Dakotas

Anyone familiar with accounts of buried treasure legends on the plains and prairies of the West knows that most such tales are set on the southern plains, and many concern Spaniards or Mexicans. Although the long history of the Spanish influence to the south is greatly responsible for such legends, the milder southern climate undoubtedly had an influence. The warmer climate in the south meant people were more active out-of-doors more months of the year than in the north, where winters are longer. Then, too, there were more people in the south than in the north.

There are not many treasure tales in what is now North Dakota, once part of Dakota Territory, perhaps for the reasons mentioned above. However, one such tale began on a summer day in the 1870s, when a Hudson's Bay Company paymaster was robbed of $40,000 in Canadian money near Estevan, Saskatchewan, on the plains of southern Canada near the U.S. border.

Sometimes there are few details about buried treasure tales, including the names of those who buried the treasures and other bits and pieces of information that are needed to make them credible. This is such a tale.

The unidentified robber fled south and crossed the Canadian border into Dakota Territory (now North Dakota), where lawmen had been alerted by the North West Mounted Police, later the Royal

Canadian Mounted Police, to watch for the robber. Dakota lawmen soon captured the robber near Big Butte, a large grass-covered hill, located about seven miles south of Lignite in what is now Burke County, North Dakota, the second county east of the Montana border. Burke County borders on the north with the Canadian province of Saskatchewan.

In those days on the frontier, lawmen were often rough on outlaws, especially if they would not talk. In this case, the lawmen beat the robber after he repeatedly refused to tell them where he had hidden the $40,000. Soon the unconscious robber was taken to the village of Portal for treatment, but the outlaw soon died of his injuries without disclosing where the money was buried.

The only clue found by lawmen was a rough diagram on the tanned side of the outlaw's fur coat. The diagram suggested that he had buried the $40,000 in the vicinity of Big Butte, which is at an altitude of 2,753 feet. Dakota lawmen searched time and again for the money but never found it. Even the North West Mounted Police reportedly crossed the border into Dakota Territory and searched the Big Butte area, but without success.

As far as anyone knows, the $40,000 is still buried somewhere on or near Big Butte.

A few years before the Canadian paymaster was robbed, something occurred in what is now Mercer County in eastern North Dakota that provides the foundation for another treasure legend. The year was 1864. A party of sixteen miners returning east from the goldfields of Montana pulled their boat ashore for repairs near where the Knife River enters the Missouri River, close to the modern site of Stanton, North Dakota.

Believing the repairs of their boat would take several days, they supposedly buried the $200,000 in gold they were carrying on the shore for safekeeping. Exactly what happened next is hazy, but a band of Indians attacked the miners. All but one of the miners were killed. The lone survivor happened to be away from camp when the Indians attacked. He hid to save his life, then fled the area after the Indians left. According to one account, he later returned in hopes of recovering the gold but never found it. Presumably, the gold is still buried where the miners left it.

Still another tale involving miners who had struck it rich in the Montana goldfields is set in what is now Burleigh County, North Dakota. During the summer of 1863, a party of twenty-four men returning east on a flatboat down the Missouri River went ashore and made camp near where Burnt Creek empties into the Missouri, about a mile north of modern Bismarck, North Dakota. Hidden on their flatboat was $90,000 in gold.

As the party made camp, an old Indian appeared. He appeared to be friendly. Although no other Indians could be seen, one miner thought he saw the old Indian signal other Indians to attack. The miner shot and killed the old Indian. Before the miners could climb back onto their flatboat and flee, a group of Indians nearby had heard the shot and rushed to the camp. Seeing the old Indian dead, they attacked and killed all of the miners.

The Indians, finding the gold hidden on the flatboat, buried it on the shore. According to one account, a portion of the gold was later recovered, but the majority of the gold is still believed to be buried where the Indians hid it.

In what is now South Dakota, one major trail used for migration, commerce, and communication ran from Deadwood in the Black Hills to Sidney in Nebraska. Stagecoaches traveled regularly over this route, carrying gold that was then shipped by train at Sidney. For more than a decade, many attempts were made to rob the stages, and some were successful.

For instance, in July 1877, a gang held up one of the stages traveling from Deadwood to Sidney at a site four miles south of Battle Creek. They supposedly fled with $200,000 in gold bullion plus items belonging to the passengers, including watches and diamonds. Because the gold was so heavy, the robbers reportedly buried it somewhere along Hat Creek south of Ardmore. There are no accounts of it ever having been found.

Pierre, South Dakota, is the setting for another treasure legend that dates back to the late 1860s or early 1870s, when an unidentified steamboat went down in the Missouri. The steamboat was reportedly carrying $500,000 in gold bullion from the mines in Montana. Details are lacking, but most accounts say that the cargo was never recovered. Soon after the steamboat sank, the Missouri River changed its course. Today the steamboat is believed to be still buried in what is now Steamboat Memorial Park at Missouri Avenue and Crow Street in Pierre. Whether the gold is still there, along with the remains of the steamboat, is anyone's guess.

The story of another Dakota buried treasure legend began in 1862. Congress, preoccupied with the Civil War, delayed appropriating funds to feed starving Sioux Indians at Yellow Medicine and Redwood Falls Indian Agencies in Minnesota, east of modern South Dakota. In the meantime, Indian traders, learning that the government would not make its customary payments to the Indians in gold coins, refused to sell the Indians any provisions on credit even though there was widespread hunger and starvation among the Indians.

On August 17, a few Indians apparently stole some eggs from a white farmer and killed five whites, including two women. The Sioux held councils, and most chose war. The next day, forty-four whites were killed at the Redwood Agency, where federal troops were trying to suppress the uprising. The following day, sixteen whites died in and around New Ulm.

During the uprising, a Dakota Sioux chief named Gray Foot and a small band of Indians stole an army payroll of about $56,000 in gold coins from an Indian agency. Gray Foot and his small band then fled into what is now Marshall County in northeastern South Dakota. The county, which borders modern North Dakota, was not organized until 1885.

The army arrested more than two thousand Sioux men, women, and children and finally restored order. By then, more than five hundred whites, including women and children, and almost fifty Dakota Sioux had been killed. Another two hundred white women and girls had been taken captive. Trials followed. Three hundred twenty-three Sioux were convicted, and three hundred three were sentenced to be hanged. However, only thirty-eight Indians were hanged, on orders from President Abraham Lincoln.

In the meantime, soldiers searched for the missing gold. In what is now South Dakota, Gray Foot heard that soldiers were sweeping the countryside, searching for the robbers and arresting any Indian who had gold coins. He did not want to be arrested, so he took his share of the stolen army payroll and buried it near the east shore of Long Lake, located east of modern Lake City, South Dakota, in what is now Marshall County.

We know this because years later, when Gray Foot was an old man and dying, he confessed to his sons how he had stolen the gold. He told them that he had buried his share and where he had buried it. After Gray Foot's death, his sons reportedly tried to locate the gold but never found it. From his sons the story spread. Other treasure seekers have searched for the gold, but there are no accounts that anyone ever found it.

11

The Virginia Dale Legend

Before the Civil War, the Butterfield Overland Stage Company followed a southerly route through Texas. When the Civil War began, the company ceased operations. Because the Union needed a safe stage route farther north, Ben Holladay started the Overland Stage Line, which followed a route from Atchison, Kansas, northwest to the Oregon Trail in Nebraska, west across Wyoming to Salt Lake City, and then to California.

When Indian raids increased along the stage lines' Oregon Trail route in Wyoming, the government ordered Holladay to shift his stage route to the south. The new route left the Oregon Trail at Julesburg, Nebraska, near the Upper California Crossing on the south bank of the South Platte River. It turned south to modern Greeley, Colorado, then a settlement called Latham, and continued to what became known as Virginia Dale and west to Fort Bridger in what is now southwest Wyoming. There the route went south to Salt Lake City.

At what became Virginia Dale, located about four miles south of the Wyoming border to the southwest of modern Cheyenne, Wyoming, Joseph A. "Jack" Slade in June 1862 built and operated the stage station for Ben Holladay. Slade called it Virginia Dale, apparently after his wife, Virginia. Little is known about Virginia other than that she was tall, handsome, and weighed about a hundred and sixty pounds.

As for Jack Slade, he was born in Carlyle, Illinois, in about 1830, give or take a year, and even as a boy had an uncontrollable temper and was easily angered. When he was thirteen, a man bothered Slade and some of his friends in Illinois. Slade reportedly picked up a rock and killed the man. His parents apparently got Slade out of town and sent him to Texas, where he later enlisted in the army in 1847 during the Mexican War. During this time, he met Virginia and they became common-law man and wife. He was not a large man, and was shorter than Virginia. After the Mexican War, Slade got a job freighting goods on the Oregon Trail. He drove a freight wagon between St. Joseph, Missouri, and the Rocky Mountains from about 1850 to 1859. He then found a job as a stagecoach driver and soon was building relay stations for the short-lived Pony Express. When Ben Holladay organized the Overland Stage Company, he was hired to build and operate the stage station that became Virginia Dale.

Benjamin Ficklin, superintendent of the Overland Stage Company, was checking the stage stations, and at Julesburg, in far northeast Colorado, more than one hundred fifty miles east of the Virginia Dale station, he discovered company property was missing. The Julesburg Station was operated by Jules Beni, who also was the line's division superintendent. Beni, a Frenchman, had hired several unsavory characters in Julesburg, a town named for him. Ficklin continued to the Virginia Dale Station and told Slade to fire Beni, get a settlement from him on the missing company property, and take over as division superintendent.

Slade rode to Julesburg and fired Beni. When he tried to get Beni to cover the cost of the missing property, Beni shot and wounded Slade with a shotgun. Slade was taken away to be treated. When Ficklin came back on the next stage and learned what had happened, he ordered Jules Beni to be hanged and left town. Friends of Jules, however, cut him down and fled, taking the Frenchman with the sore neck with them.

After Jack Slade recovered, he went after Jules Beni and found him. It is unclear where Beni was located, but Slade shot him in the thigh, then tied Beni to a corral post and used him for target practice until the next morning. Beni pleaded for Slade to kill him. Slade walked up to Beni and shot him dead. Before the body with a reported twenty-two bullet wounds was taken away for burial, Slade supposedly took his knife and sliced off Beni's ears. One account says Slade used one ear as a watch fob. Another says he had fun walking up to a bar, tossing down the ear, and asking for change.

Slade liked to drink. When sober, he was a gentle and good-natured person. When drunk, however, he was dangerous. Mark Twain, traveling across country by stage, had heard stories about Slade. Twain stopped at Virginia Dale for breakfast along with, as he wrote, "a half-savage, half-civilized company of armed and bearded mountaineers, ranchmen and station employees."

In his book *Roughing It* (1872), Twain added:

> The most gentlemanly appearing, quiet and affable officer we had yet found along the road in the Overland Company's service was the person who sat at the head of the table, at my elbow. Never youth stared and shivered as I did when I heard them call him SLADE!
>
> Here was romance, and I sitting face to face with it! . . . looking upon it . . . touching it . . . hobnobbing with it, as it were! Here, right by my side, was the actual ogre who, in fights and brawls and various ways, had taken the lives of twenty-six human beings, or all men lied about him! I suppose I was the proudest stripling that ever traveled to see strange lands and wonderful people.
>
> He was so friendly and so gentle-spoken that I warmed to him in spite of his awful history. . . . The coffee ran out. At least it was reduced to one tin-cupful, and Slade was about to take it when he saw that my cup was empty. He politely offered to fill it, but although I wanted it, I politely declined. I was afraid he had not killed anybody that morning, and might be needing diversion.

Jack's wife Virginia managed to keep her husband in line much of the time, but when he was away from her, he often went on drunken sprees. He narrowly missed being fired during one such spree in Denver. Then there was the incident at Fort Halleck, a post constructed by the army in 1862 near Elk Mountain in modern-day Wyoming to protect the stagecoaches from Indian attacks.

A drunken Slade went into the sutler's store at Fort Halleck and used the canned goods on the shelves for target practice, then caused general mayhem. The commanding officer arrested Slade and refused to release him until Ben Holladay promised that he would fire Slade.

This drawing from Mark Twain's
Roughing It (1872) shows Twain
(right) politely declining the last cup
of coffee offered by Jack Slade (left).
(Author's Collection)

About that time, an Overland Stage Company coach carrying an army payroll of $60,000 in ten- and twenty-dollar gold coins for Fort Sanders, Wyoming Territory, was robbed by six masked men on Long View Hill, a mile or two from the Virginia Dale Station.

The outlaws fled west with the strongbox until they reached the tree-covered foothills of the nearby mountains. There they stopped, shot the lock off, and took the gold coins. By then, however, they heard soldiers following in pursuit. The outlaws supposedly buried the heavy gold coins, likely because of the weight. The soldiers, however, soon caught up with the outlaws and killed all six. The army never recovered the gold.

The robbery was one of many that occurred in the area around Virginia Dale, but this time, the robbers had been caught and killed. Many people suspected Jack Slade was their ringleader, but they had no proof. When Slade was fired for the incident at Fort Halleck, he left Virginia Dale peacefully with his wife. To everyone's surprise, Slade held his temper and seemed pleased to leave.

Slade and Virginia bought a small ranch near Virginia City, Montana. After getting settled in their new home, Slade went into Virginia City, got drunk, and wrecked a saloon. He supposedly said he would pay for the damages, but he had spent his money on whiskey. The local vigilantes' committee issued a warrant for his arrest. When he was handed the warrant, Slade tore it up and made threats. The vigilantes took Jack Slade out and hanged him on March 10, 1864.

When his wife on their nearby ranch learned what had happened, she rushed into Virginia City on horseback, cussing the townspeople loudly. The vigilantes threatened to hang her if she did not take Jack's body and get out of town. She made quick arrangements with the town's undertaker, bought a metal casket, and took Jack Slade's body back to the ranch. There she pickled her husband's body in alcohol and reportedly kept it in the metal casket under her bed for some time. A few months later, she packed her belongings and, along with the coffin, took a stage to Salt Lake City. There Jack Slade was buried in the old city cemetery, Block B, Lot 6, Grave 7. His grave marker can be seen today.

It is still not known whether Jack Slade was the leader of the outlaws who stole the $60,000 in gold coins near Virginia Dale in 1863, but those coins have never been recovered and may still be buried somewhere near the Virginia Dale stage station, which still survives.

12

Did Henry Starr Leave a Buried Treasure?

If the words of Henry Starr can be trusted, this outlaw, whose crimes bridged the nineteenth and early twentieth centuries, left a buried treasure in far southwest Kansas. The truth of this legend rests with Starr's credibility, and to get a sense of what that may have been, one must examine his life.

Henry Starr was born on December 2, 1873, at Fort Gibson in eastern Indian Territory, now Oklahoma. His father, George "Hop" Starr, was a half-breed Cherokee. His mother, Mary Scot, who was one-quarter Cherokee, had Irish ancestry. She came from an educated and respectable family. Henry's father, however, came from a family full of unsavory characters. Henry's grandfather, Tom Starr, was an outlaw, and Henry's uncle was Sam Starr, an outlaw who married another outlaw, the famous Belle Starr.

Young Henry Starr grew up in what may have been the most lawless part of Indian Territory, the area from Fort Gibson northward to the Kansas border and eastward to Arkansas. The northeastern part of Indian Territory was full of outlaws, many of whom had fled to the Indian nation to avoid the law. At the time, there was no extradition for criminals caught in Indian Territory.

When Henry Starr was about thirteen, his father died, leaving his mother the tasks of raising three children and running the family

66

farm. She soon remarried, and C. N. Walker became Henry's stepfather. They did not get along. Henry did not think he was a good man. Then, too, his new stepfather was not an Indian. The boy and his stepfather frequently argued, and Henry was beaten. He soon ran away from home.

Henry had his first run-in with the law when he was about eighteen. He was working on a ranch when lawmen arrested him for stealing another man's horse. As Henry later wrote in his autobiography *Thrilling Events* (1914), the horse had wandered onto the ranch where Henry was working. He took care of the animal for about a month until the owner came by and claimed the horse. Henry wrote that the owner thanked him profusely for taking care of the horse, but after the man left, he swore out a warrant for Henry Starr's arrest.

Starr was taken before Judge Isaac Parker's court in Fort Smith, Arkansas, and remained in jail until the charges were dismissed for lack of evidence. Starr was free, but the short time he was behind bars changed him. He lost respect for the law. As he rode his horse back into Indian Territory, he said he thought about how one could beat the law.

Soon Starr and two other young men, Ed Newcome and Jesse Jackson, decided to rob a railroad depot at Nowata, Indian Territory. In June 1892, they escaped with $1,700, but Starr's identity was soon discovered. He was arrested and taken back to Fort Smith, where Starr pleaded "not guilty." Released on $2,000 bond, he quickly returned to Indian Territory, determined never to return to Judge Parker's court.

When Starr did not appear in court at Fort Smith, Deputy U.S. Marshal Floyd Wilson was sent to bring him in. On December 14, 1892, Wilson found Starr in Nenapah and called to him to stop. Starr apparently yelled he would not, and gunfire erupted. The facts are hazy, but according to Starr's recollections, Wilson and another lawman fired first. Starr fired back, he said, in self-defense. Wilson fell to the ground. The other lawman some distance away played possum. Starr walked up to Wilson and fired several more bullets into the body. From what evidence has been found, Wilson was the only person Starr killed during his life of crime.

Starr quickly rode off and soon teamed up with Frank Cheney, a farmer living near Wagoner, Indian Territory. They made off with more than four hundred dollars when they robbed the train depot and two stores in Choteau, and within a few days they held up the depot and a store at Inola for another four hundred dollars.

But these robberies did not produce much cash. When Starr and Cheney returned to the Osage Hills, Starr decided they should rob a bank. He began analyzing how to rob a bank and concluded that daylight hours were best, and a large gang should not be used. In March 1893, he put his strategy to use. Starr and Cheney crossed the border into Kansas and rode into the town of Caney. It was raining, and there were few people on the street. They walked into the Caney National Bank and drew their revolvers. While Starr watched the employees, Cheney went into the vault and filled a bushel sack with money. They locked the employees in a back room and fled back across the border into Indian Territory. When they were nearly a hundred miles back into Indian Territory, the two men stopped to count their loot. They had gotten away with more than $5,000. Cheney apparently returned to farming, but Henry Starr was becoming a wanted man.

Starr realized that there was more money in robbing banks. About three months later, on June 5, 1893, he rode into Bentonville in northwest Arkansas. This time, he had four men with him, including one known as Kid Wilson. Starr was recognized before they reached the People's Bank. Inside they took as much money as they could carry until they heard gunfire outside the bank. Starr, Kid Wilson, and the other outlaws fled as fast as they could, only to be chased by a posse. The robbers, however, managed to escape. When they eventually stopped to rest, they counted the money. They had gotten away with $11,999. But when Starr divided the loot between the gang, each member only had slightly more than $2,000.

Starr was blamed for the Bentonville bank robbery, and he became even more of a wanted man. Lawmen distributed wanted posters, some of which included Starr's photograph. He realized he was not safe in public, and with Kid Wilson and a lady friend, the trio rode north into Kansas. At Emporia, they boarded a train, intending to travel west to California. When they reached Colorado Springs, Colorado, the trio decided to stop and see the sights. Starr was recognized, and four policemen arrested him, along with Kid Wilson.

On July 13, 1893, lawmen left Colorado to return Starr and Wilson to Fort Smith to stand trial. Starr faced one count of murder and thirteen counts of highway robbery. Starr's trial focused on his killing of the deputy U.S. marshal. He was found guilty and sentenced to die on the gallows. The case was appealed, and Starr's sentence was commuted by the United States Supreme Court and a new trial granted.

On July 26, 1895, while waiting in the Fort Smith jail for his second trial, another prisoner, an outlaw named Crawford Goldsby, alias Cherokee Bill, killed a guard and barricaded himself in a cell in an attempt to break jail. Starr, who was an old friend of Cherokee Bill's, offered to talk him into surrendering. Prison officials took him up on his offer. Starr reached Goldsby, convinced him to give Starr his revolver, and give up. Starr gave the gun to the guards.

Soon Starr's second trial was held, and again, he was found guilty of murder and sentenced to die. The case was again appealed to the U.S. Supreme Court, where Judge Isaac Parker and Justice Edward White engaged in a war of words. White accused Parker of abusing his power. Parker accused White of not knowing the law. The Supreme Court overturned Starr's conviction and granted him a third trial.

Before the third trail could be held in Judge Parker's Fort Smith court, the judge died in November 1896. In Starr's third trial, held early in 1897, he pleaded guilty to manslaughter and was given three years in jail. For his other crimes, Starr was given seven years and seven days in jail. Starr was then taken to the federal prison at Columbus, Ohio, where he was a model prisoner.

Soon after the twentieth century began, Starr's mother went to Washington, D.C., and was granted an interview with President Theodore Roosevelt. She told her son's story. Roosevelt wired Starr and asked him if he would behave himself if he were pardoned. Starr said yes, that he was determined to follow the straight and narrow path. Starr was pardoned in January 1903 after serving only three years of a fifteen-year sentence.

Henry Starr returned to Tulsa, where his mother owned a restaurant. Starr married, and he and his wife had a child they named Theodore Roosevelt Starr. He felt like a free man until he learned that authorities in Arkansas were seeking his extradition to stand trial for the 1893 Bentonville bank robbery. Starr later wrote that he would rather be in a cemetery than spend the rest of his life on an Arkansas convict farm.

Starr again turned to robbing banks. With Kid Wilson, he robbed the State Bank at Tyro, Kansas, and then headed for California. When they reached Amity, Colorado, they found a bank that "looked too good to pass up," according to Starr. They got away with $1,100 and split up. What happened to Kid Wilson is not known, but Starr spent the summer and fall of 1908 hiding in New Mexico. He wrote a letter to a friend in Tulsa, but the friend apparently betrayed him. On May 11, 1909, lawmen located Starr and arrested him for the Colorado bank robbery, tried him, and sent him to state prison at Canon City, Colorado.

Again, he was a model prisoner and was soon made a trustee. It was in the Colorado prison that Starr wrote *Thrilling Events: The Life of Henry Starr.* In 1914, he was paroled on the condition that he never leave Colorado. Starr promised he would not and was released. He quickly returned to Oklahoma, where the book he had written in prison was printed in Tulsa. Between September 8, 1914, and January 13, 1815—a period of about four months—Starr robbed fourteen different banks. Each bank was robbed during daylight hours. That was about one robbery every two weeks. The total take in all of the robberies was more than $26,000.

The Oklahoma legislature soon passed the "Bank Robber Bill," offering a reward of $15,000 for the capture of bank robbers plus a $1,000 bounty on each robber, dead or alive. While lawmen searched the Osage Hills for Starr, he was living comfortably only two blocks from the sheriff's office in Tulsa. It was there he apparently decided to do what the Dalton Gang had failed to accomplish in 1892 at Coffeyville, Kansas. Starr was going to rob two banks at the same time, and he made plans to do so in Stroud, a town located about fifty miles northeast of Oklahoma City.

Starr put together a gang of eight men and sent a letter to the governor of Oklahoma denying he had any part in the robberies and saying he had been in Nevada when they occurred. This was undoubtedly a lie. Then Starr left Tulsa with his gang and arrived in Stroud about a week before the robbery was planned. The gang camped two miles east of town on a farm owned by George Rogers. On Saturday morning, March 27, 1915, the eight men rode their horses into Stroud to the stockyards and tied their horses to a fence. One member of the gang watched the horses while the seven remaining members divided into two groups.

Starr and two men headed for the Stroud National Bank while the four other outlaws walked to the First National Bank, one block away from the other bank. At the Stroud National Bank, Starr left one man outside the door on guard. As Starr and another outlaw entered the bank, they noticed on the front door a reward poster for Starr and his gang. They said nothing, but as they entered, they drew their revolvers and announced that it was a hold-up. Inside, there were three men: Lee Patrick, vice president; J. B. Charles, bookkeeper; and J. M. Reed, a customer. Patrick was taken to a back room by an outlaw while Starr went behind the cage, where the bookkeeper sat at his desk. Starr tossed him a sack and told him to fill it. The bookkeeper filled it with currency and silver and gave it to Starr, who noticed there was more silver on the counter. Starr gave the bookkeeper another sack and told him to fill it, which he did. The outlaw who was standing outside the front door joined Starr and the others in the bank. The three bandits marched the customer and two bank employees out the back door of the bank and down an alley until they came within sight of the other bank.

In the meantime, the four other outlaws had entered the First National Bank. There were seven people inside—five bank employees and two customers—when the outlaws entered and announced it was a hold-up. One of the outlaws slipped a Winchester rifle from under his coat and went to the rear of the bank. Another outlaw closed the front door and stood guard. A third outlaw walked up and down in front of the cage, while the fourth walked behind the cage and thumped the butt of his rife on the floor and demanded the money and gold.

The fourth outlaw tossed an empty sack to the cashier, who went into the vault and put $4,500 into it. More than $2,300 of the money was gold. The cashier told the outlaws that was all the money they had and that "you might as well go." One of the outlaws replied, "No, we'll be ready in a minute. We're going to wait for the other boys up the street. We are taking both banks in today."

The two bunches of outlaws soon met outside the First National Bank, and with their prisoners, they headed to the stockyards and their horses. By then, however, the townspeople, learning of the robberies, were looking for their weapons. Before the outlaws reached their horses, Starr warned a bystander to get back. When Walter Martin, a farmer, froze instead of retreating, Starr fired at him, wounding the man in the shoulder.

It was then that a teenager, Paul Curry, the son of a grocer armed with a short-barrel rifle used by a butcher to kill hogs, fired at Starr. The bullet struck Starr in the leg, and he collapsed against a wire fence, then fell to the ground. Curry shouted at Starr, "Throw your gun away or I'll kill you." Starr did as he was told. Curry went over to Starr as townspeople arrived to help. Starr was carried to a doctor's office located above one of the banks. Starr's leg bone was shattered close to the hip. He did not flinch while the doctor was dressing it. Starr told the doctor that he could take his horse and saddle in payment for his medical services.

Meanwhile, the other outlaws had reached their horses, mounted, and were riding low to the horses' necks as fast as they could go while townspeople fired at them, until the outlaws rode over the crest of a hill. Two armed men followed them in a motor car. Two miles out of town, the two men found one of the outlaws, Lewis Estes, leaning against a tree. He raised one hand to indicate surrender. He was taken back to Stroud and the doctor's office where Starr was being treated.

The six remaining outlaws escaped. After the doctor treated Starr and Estes, they were taken to the county seat at Chandler, Oklahoma, and jailed. Later Starr stood trial and on August 2, 1915, pleaded guilty to the Stroud robbery. He was sentenced to twenty-five years in prison at the Oklahoma State Penitentiary at McAlester.

Again Starr, now forty-five, was a model prisoner, and he spoke of his foolishness in following a life of crime. Interviews with newspaper reporters had the desired effect, and he was paroled on March 15, 1919. For two years, he lived an honest life and got into the silent motion picture business. He produced and starred in *A Debtor to the Law*. This film depicted the Stroud bank robberies and the senselessness of becoming a criminal.

Starr went on to produce two other movies, and he even received an offer from Hollywood to do a movie there. He turned the

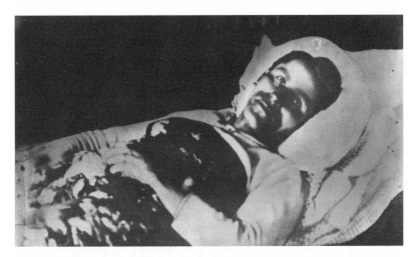

On March 27, 1915, Henry Starr and his gang tried to rob two banks in Stroud, Oklahoma. Starr was wounded and arrested. This photograph shows Starr in a Stroud doctor's office recovering from his wounds. (Courtesy Western History Collections, University of Oklahoma Libraries)

offer down, fearing that Arkansas authorities might try to extradite him for the Bentonville bank robbery years before. During this period, he married again, and with his bride, he moved to Claremore, Oklahoma.

Starr could not take a dull and honest life. He apparently missed the excitement and adventure of robbing banks. On Friday, February 18, 1921, Starr and three other men, driving a high-powered touring car, drove into Harrison in north-central Arkansas and robbed a bank. As Starr was gathering money in the vault, W. J. Myers, a former president of the bank, grabbed a Winchester rifle in a corner and shot Starr in the back. The other outlaws fled. Starr was carried to the jail, where a doctor removed the bullet. Starr, however, was critically wounded.

Starr lingered. On Monday, three days after the robbery, he boasted to those with him that he had robbed more banks than any man in America. By then his wife and son had arrived at the jail from Claremore. The following morning, Tuesday, February 21, 1921, Starr died.

This photograph of Henry Starr
was taken in Tulsa, Oklahoma, in
1919. (Courtesy Western History
Collections, University of
Oklahoma Libraries)

His wife told a newspaper reporter that her husband had a pre-monition of his death. "Just before he left me at Claremore last Wednesday, Henry called me to him and put his arm around me. 'Honey,' he said, 'if I died would you have me buried?' 'Of course I would,' I told him. 'Why?' 'Well,' he said, 'because I don't want to be buried into the ground. I want to be cremated.' A little later he kissed me goodbye and walked hurried away, without looking back."

Henry Starr's remains were buried at Dewey, Oklahoma. Whether or not his body was cremated is not known, but his grave has no marker. It is next to a grave with a headstone reading "Baby Starr."

It is not known whether Henry Starr ever discussed with any of his wives or son his public claim that he buried loot from his early robberies "near the border in a place nobody could find it in a million years." He apparently made that statement while in the Colorado State Penitentiary. Many treasure hunters have tried to find the location of that treasure, which may amount to several thousand dollars, perhaps in gold coins. The strongest speculation is that if Starr buried a treasure, as he said he did, it is probably located somewhere along the Cimarron River in northwest Stevens County, the extreme southwest county in Kansas. He is known to have been in that region early in the twentieth century.

Was Henry Starr telling the truth? Did he bury some of his early loot? These questions remain unanswered.

13

The Stage Station Treasure

In 1850, the first regular mail service was established between Independence, Missouri, and Santa Fe. David Waldo, a medical doctor at Independence and a Santa Fe trader, obtained a four-year contract to carry the mail once a month between the two places. He used the carriages belonging to Waldo, Hall and Company, which he owned with Jacob Hall and William McCoy, men with considerable experience in the Santa Fe trade.

As two carriages traversed the Santa Fe Trail, one from Independence and another starting from Santa Fe, each was guarded by eight men. Each man was armed with a Colt rifle, a Colt revolver, and a hunting knife. The *Missouri Commonwealth*, in reporting the new mail service, noted that if the guards were attacked, they could discharge "one hundred and thirty-six shots without stopping to load. This is equal to a small army armed as in ancient times, and from the looks of this escort, ready as they are for either offensive or defensive warfare with the savages, we have no fears for the safety of the mails."

David Waldo retained the mail contract until 1858, when Jacob Hall obtained it after promising to deliver the mail between Independence, Missouri, and Santa Fe twice a month. The firm of Hall and Porter began running a monthly line of wagons between St. Louis and Santa Fe. The route followed what has became known as the mountain route of the Santa Fe Trail. Hall soon added a passenger service. For two hundred fifty dollars, a person could travel the more than seven hundred miles between the two towns. The company used various kinds of wagons, especially the ambulance type, and not the customary stagecoach that later appeared in the West. Thus passenger comfort was not always good.

Hall and Porter's business became so popular that the eastern terminus was moved from St. Louis to Independence, Missouri, and later carried the mail and passengers on a weekly basis, making the seven-hundred-mile trip to Santa Fe in about fifteen days.

During the late 1860s, the stage line between Kansas City and Santa Fe was controlled by Colonel J. L. Sanderson. One of the company's stage stations was located at Fort Aubry, about halfway between Medway and Syracuse on the Santa Fe Trail near the Arkansas River in southwest Kansas.

Fort Aubry began as Camp Wynkoop, established in May 1864 to watch for Confederate rebels and to check Indian movements with one company of soldiers. In the fall of 1864, it became Fort Aubry and was staffed by two companies of Missouri volunteer cavalry and two companies of Wisconsin volunteer infantrymen. These troops were assigned the task of escorting stage line wagons and freighters between Fort Dodge, about a hundred miles to the east, to Fort Lyon, Colorado Territory.

Fort Aubry was not much of a fort and consisted mainly of dugouts. In January 1866, the volunteer troops were replaced by regular army men, one company of cavalry and one company of infantry. Then in April 1866, the government abandoned Fort Aubry. The stage line from Kansas City to Santa Fe continued to use the abandoned post as a stage station.

It was in 1867 that Felix Goldman had the job of operating the state station for the company's weekly runs. One day, a tough-looking character began to visit the station daily. In Goldman's mind, the man, who appeared friendly, asked too many questions and scrutinized Goldman and the station too much.

Goldman sent a message to his supervisor. He described the appearance and actions of the suspicious man, but informed his supervisor that he had buried his own savings and the station's operating funds, which totaled about $17,000 in gold and silver. He said he made certain no one saw where he buried it.

When the weekly stage run arrived at the station a few days later, the driver found Goldman dead. He had been murdered. A search of the stage station turned up nothing. Lawmen, which probably included a U.S. marshal, used Goldman's written description of the suspicious character as they searched the area, and they arrested a man named Tolliver who fit the description. Tolliver, however, swore he had not killed Goldman, nor had he taken anything from the stage station. The lawmen apparently released Tolliver because they had no evidence that he had killed Goldman.

From all accounts, the buried treasure was never found. It raises the possibility that the treasure remains buried somewhere in the vicinity of the old stage station halfway between Medway and Syracuse on U.S. Highway 50 in modern Hamilton County, Kansas, near the Colorado border and two counties north of the Oklahoma line. Only a few signs remain of the dugouts that were once Fort Aubry and the stage station.

14

The Sheepherder's Treasure

The rolling plains of Young County in north-central Texas is the setting for this tale about a Mexican who raised sheep. The man, not identified by name, set up a camp after the Civil War some distance from Fort Belknap, a military post, located three miles south of the town of Newcastle. The fort was founded in June 1851 and abandoned in September 1867. It was the northernmost anchor of a chain of forts stretching from the Rio Grande north to the Red River and was built to protect the Texas frontier.

The Mexican apparently came to the area just after Fort Belknap was abandoned, when fewer than two hundred people lived in what is now Young County. Very little is known about the Mexican other than that he was a shady character with little regard for the law and what is right. He owned about two thousand sheep and hired two herders to care for the animals. One was a Mexican boy in his teens. The other was a grown man in the forties.

The Mexican's sheep camp consisted of a dugout, an excavation in a high bank facing a creek about one hundred feet away. On each side of the dugout was a corral. From the outside of each corral was a stone wall that ran from the bank down to the creek and was connected by another stone wall that ran along the edge of the creek. Each night the sheep were put inside the stone wall. The two herders slept along the edge of the creek while their employer slept in the dugout.

One night, the herders had finished putting the sheep inside the stone wall and were sitting by the creek when their employer had a visitor with three packhorses. The herders watched as their employer helped the visitor carry three heavy saddlebags into the dugout. In the morning, the visitor left, but he returned about a month later, loaded the saddlebags back onto his horses, and left before dawn. A few months later the visitor returned, and three more saddlebags were carried into the dugout. The visitor then left.

By now, the two herders suspected that the saddlebags contained gold and that their employer had other business interests. A few hours later, the man and teenager crept into the dugout, murdered their employer, dragged the body outside, and buried it in a shallow grave. Back inside the dugout, they found that one saddlebag contained $110,000 in U.S. gold coins. Each took about $4,000 in gold and then buried the remaining $102,000.

The next morning, the two herders, riding one horse, left the sheep to survive on their own and rode south, toward the Rio Grande. A couple of nights later, the teenager demanded that they go back and get the rest of the gold. The man tried to convince him to leave the buried gold—that they simply could not carry it. When he was unsuccessful, the man killed the boy, took his $4,000 in gold, and continued toward old Mexico on the one horse.

He made it across the Rio Grande and kept going until he reached a fair-sized city in Mexico. There he began spending his gold freely. He drank and gambled and chased women. When one señorita's boyfriend challenged the attention the man was showing the woman, the drunken former sheepherder shot the fellow. He was quickly arrested, tried, and given a life sentence at hard labor in a Mexican prison.

The years passed, and the one-time herder aged. He then got sick. Because he could no longer work, the Mexican authorities granted him a reprieve and set him free. He began to make plans to go north to dig up the buried gold in Texas, but his health was too poor to travel. He saw a doctor, who told him he must operate.

It was then that the one-time herder told the doctor the story that has been related. He told the doctor where the gold was buried, and he promised that as soon as the operation was over and he could travel, he would take the doctor with him and they would divide the gold. The man died on the operating table, however, and he was buried in a pauper's grave.

The unidentified doctor later went to Texas and tried to locate the gold. When he could not find it, he returned to Mexico, leaving written instructions with a friend on where the gold was buried.

The unidentified friend later shared the document with Robert G. Ferguson, a native of Arkansas born in 1875. Ferguson put the story on paper, describing the sheepherder's camp and indicating that the gold was buried about a furlong from the dugout on the bank of the creek. As to the camp's location, it was on an unidentified creek supposedly about a two-day journey by burro from Fort Belknap, but no direction was given. This would likely put the sheep camp about twenty miles from the abandoned military post. It is not known whether the location of the sheepherder's camp has ever been found, or whether anyone found the gold that was supposedly buried there.

15

Legend of "The Cave"

It has been estimated that there are about eight hundred natural caves in Kansas, thanks to underlying limestone in many areas of the state. It is believed that most of the natural caves were formed about two hundred million years ago by water erosion and aquifers that rise and fall with seasonal rains. One such cave is located six miles south and one mile west of Hope in Dickinson County, Kansas.

"The Cave," as local residents refer to it, holds many mysteries, but unfortunately, years ago, the entrance collapsed, making it nearly impossible for anyone to solve them. Its location, however—only three miles north of the old Santa Fe Trail, a few miles east of the Chisholm Trail, and close to a military trail from Fort Leavenworth and Fort Riley, Kansas, to where it joined the Santa Fe Trail—suggests many possibilities for its use in the nineteenth century.

Abilene, the first cattle town in Kansas, is about twenty-three miles north-northwest. From Abilene south through Dickinson and Marion Counties, the Chisholm Trail ran through undulating prairie. Beginning in 1867, herds of Texas longhorns were driven north to the railhead market in Abilene until fall 1871. By then, settlers had moved into the region south of Abilene, including a group of about forty people from Michigan. As the community that became Hope grew, a post office was established in 1871. The town's first business building was a general store called the Roundhouse, built by Newell

Thurstin. It appears he named the settlement Hope after one of his sons. As Hope grew and southern Dickinson County was settled, remains of the Chisholm Trail disappeared as the land was tilled and crops planted. As settlers got to know each other and socialized, someone familiar with the Cave told others about its existence. Some settlers may have gone to inspect it. If so, they left little information about it. In time, stories about the Cave were handed down from generation to generation like much local history everywhere.

In the 1990s, Hope historian Larry Potter heard stories about the Cave and in a history of his community wrote, "It was large enough a horse could be led into it and long enough that when a fire was lit near the entrance smoke could be seen three miles north. Reportedly one fellow went in one day and came out several days later near Gypsum, about twenty miles west."

Old-timers told Potter that they remembered hearing stories about gold having been hidden in the Cave. Some said it was hidden by returning gold seekers who had followed the gold rush to California and struck it rich. When they were returning east, apparently following the Santa Fe Trail, they were attacked by Indians and at least one man escaped, fled north to the Cave, and supposedly hid the gold. Other old-timers said gold was hidden by outlaws who had stolen a military payroll being taken by soldiers following the military trail from either Fort Leavenworth or Fort Riley to other military posts, perhaps including Fort Union, New Mexico.

The old-timers apparently could not remember the exact details, if any gold was in fact lost. Still, the stories persisted. Dickinson County was surveyed in 1857, and by 1860 there were 368 people living there. Whether or not they knew of the Cave is not known, but there were no roads in the country, only a few trails, some made by buffalo. Settlers were probably too busy trying to survive off the land to spend much time investigating the Cave.

If gold was hidden in the Cave, it probably occurred before the Civil War, when there were few people living in what became Dickinson County. Had people taken up residence there, some record probably would have been left. A search of early recollections of travelers in the region and reminiscences of old-timers turned up nothing.

There is always the possibility that when the Cave was discovered by early settlers, one of them might have wondered aloud if any gold was hidden there. At the time, stories of buried treasure were popular, and western gold rushes in California and what is now Colorado were recent events. The idea could have been taken as fact, and the legend was born. Because the entrance to the Cave collapsed some years ago and it remains on private property, we may never know whether there is any truth to the legend. Still, the stories persist and remain a good subject for conversation on hot summer days or cold winter nights.

16

The Lost Treasure of the Missouri Traders

The skies were clear and it was cold that December day in 1832 when a party of twelve traders left Santa Fe for their Missouri homes. The traders rode horses and led a mule pack-train carrying supplies and between $10,000 and $12,000 in gold and silver, profits from their trading ventures. Judge John H. Carr reportedly led the party as they moved east, and others in the party may have been Thomas Eustace, Washington Chapman, and John Harris.

The men were dressed warmly for the winter weather, but the sun warmed them from about midmorning until midafternoon as they headed east. The nights, however, were cold. Their journey was uneventful as they moved into what is now the Texas Panhandle, following the Canadian River, the largest tributary of the Arkansas River, which rises in the Sangre de Cristo Mountains near modern Raton, New Mexico. They had traveled about two hundred miles from Santa Fe when on January 1, 1833, perhaps two hundred Indians, either Kiowa or Comanche or both, began harassing the traders, approaching them in small groups first from one side and then another. Not trusting the Indians, the traders hurriedly moved their horses and mules into a circle near one or more trees along the river's edge and quickly dug a long, deep trench in the sandy soil for protection. Suddenly the Indians began firing their weapons at the traders, who returned fire.

Within minutes, two traders were killed. One man named Pratt was hit and fell dead while trying to catch two mules that broke loose and ran. The other man, named Mitchell, who was from Boone County, Missouri, was shot and killed. One trader was hit, but it was a flesh wound and not serious. From the protection of their trench, the Missourians fought off the Indians until dark, when their attackers stopped fighting and withdrew a short distance from the traders. By then, all of the traders' horses and mules were dead or wounded. The animal's bodies provided additional protection for the traders. The Missourians rested as best they could, trying to keep warm, and discussed their predicament. With no horses or mules, they knew they could not carry all of the heavy gold and silver. Each man took what gold and silver he could carry on his person, and the rest was buried in the sandy soil and carefully covered so their cache would not be noticeable. About midnight, they decided to escape under cover of darkness. They quietly left their camp, but they did not get far. Indians spotted them trying to escape and drove them back to their makeshift camp.

The traders rested and waited for dawn, knowing the Indians would again attack. They did as the light of a new day could be seen on the eastern horizon. The on-and-off fighting continued into late afternoon. By then, the traders' ammunition was almost gone, and they feared the worst. Suddenly, the Indians stopped fighting. Some distance from the traders, an Indian yelled in Spanish, telling the traders they could go.

The traders were surprised as they watched the Indians leave the area and disappear over the horizon. Thinking it might be a trick, the traders waited in camp and tried to rest and keep warm, ever watchful for another attack. But none came. At dawn, there were no Indians to be seen. Why the Indians had given up was not clear. It could have been the cold weather, or the fact that all of the traders' horses and mules, which were valuable to the Indians, had been killed. Regardless, the traders set out, carrying what gold and silver they had in their pockets and carrying what supplies they could.

For reasons that are unclear, the traders soon divided into two groups. One group of five started east, following the Canadian River in hopes of reaching a Creek Indian settlement. The other five men took the most direct route east, probably following the Santa Fe Trail. Those taking the direct route east reached Missouri safely. As for the five men who followed the Canadian River, it took forty-two days to reach the Creek Indian settlement in what is now central Oklahoma, but only three of the five men in the group made it. Two of the men, including one identified as William R. Schenck, apparently could not keep up with the others, gave up, and died from starvation and cold. With no ammunition, they could not kill game for food.

How much gold and silver the traders left buried near the Canadian River is not known. One unconfirmed report suggests that some Mexican traders may have found the gold and silver because later they were seen freely spending money. Most accounts, however, suggest that the gold and silver were never found. Unfortunately for modern treasure hunters, details are vague as to the exact spot where the traders buried the gold and silver. Most have speculated that the site is somewhere along the Canadian River north or northwest of modern Amarillo, Texas, but the exact location is not known.

Part III

THE LAWLESS, LAWMEN, AND JUSTICE

He reminds me of the man who murdered both his parents, and then when sentence was about to be pronounced pleaded for mercy on the grounds that he was an orphan.
—Abraham Lincoln

17

Civilizing No-Man's-Land

Dodge City, Abilene, Tascosa, and Deadwood are some of the towns that come to mind when one thinks of lawlessness in the Old West. The truth is, the town of Beaver in the no-man's-land between southwest Kansas and the Texas Panhandle may have been for a short time the most lawless place on the plains between Texas and North Dakota. Congress had a hand in making it so until settlers brought law and order and civilization to the region.

To understand how this happened, one must go back to the Compromise of 1850, when the United States acquired a vast amount of land that Texas had claimed since its days as a republic. When Texas joined the Union as a slave state, it agreed not to extend its sovereignty over any territory north of 36 degrees and 30 seconds north. Thus the Panhandle of Texas only stretched that far north, even though as a republic, Texas claimed a strip of land stretching northward into modern Wyoming.

When Kansas Territory was created in 1854, its southern boundary was set on the thirty-seventh parallel, an east-west line agreed to in the Missouri Compromise of 1820 that called for all territory north of that line to be free and everything south to be slave. This left a narrow strip of land about thirty-four miles wide and about one hundred sixty-eight miles long between Kansas and the Texas Panhandle. No state claimed the land, and maps came to identify it simply as "Public Land Strip."

Indians occasionally camped there, traders following the Cimarron Cutoff on the Santa Fe Trail crossed the western end, and parties of U.S. troops crossed the strip, but it was unsettled. The sand dunes, sagebrush, and grasslands were as inhospitable to visitors as was the summer heat on the treeless open country that climbed from two thousand feet in the east to four thousand feet on the west near the New Mexico border.

The barren strip did not seem to offer anything for humans but desolation until about 1878, when hostile Indians were moved to reservations. Texas ranchers realized the grazing potential of the rich grasslands in the strip, started ranches, established loose ranch boundaries by consensus, and let their cattle graze on the open range. These cattlemen got their supplies from the towns of Mobeetie and Tascosa in Texas or from Dodge City to the north in Kansas.

Jim Lane, who had freighted supplies across the strip, was apparently the first permanent settler in the strip. About 1880, he brought several wagons loaded with supplies along with his family and pitched camp near a grove of large cottonwood trees on the south bank of the Beaver River. He then constructed a large dugout with three rooms: one for himself and his family, another for a store, and one for visitors.

In time, Lane brought doors and window frames from Dodge City, along with windowpanes, and improved his dugout. He also added a stove to heat his family's room. He kept a good supply of tobacco, bacon, coffee, beans, flour, ammunition, and other goods to sell to cowboys and others traveling through the area.

Other settlers in the strip were scarce until 1885, when the U.S. land office commissioner in Washington affirmed that the strip was not part of Indian Territory but was federal public lands subject to squatter's rights. The news spread like a prairie fire, and land-hungry settlers suffering from drought and economic depression in nearby states, especially western Kansas, left their heavily mortgaged farms and headed into the strip.

Finding no land office or government surveys, they surveyed the land into quarter sections and referred to "zinc pot" markers left by surveyors at two-mile intervals along six-mile-square congressional townships across the strip that were surveyed in 1881. The settlers

This settler's sod house was located in what is today eastern Beaver County of the Oklahoma Panhandle. Photograph by F. M. Steel. (Courtesy Kansas State Historical Society)

then squatted on their claims, thinking that in time, they could acquire legal title. Because they were poor and could not afford seed and expensive equipment, they had gardens and raised only what they needed to survive.

Because there was no territorial or state government overseeing the strip, each community of squatters set up its own irregular government, including courts and schools, and established vigilante committees to enforce order. A few settlements even hired men to enforce the law.

Vigilante justice, however, prevailed. In one instance, cattlemen caught three cattle rustlers at the settlement of Sod Town southeast of Beaver, tried them in a vigilance committee court, and sentenced them to death by hanging. Because there were no trees in the area, members of the vigilance committee propped up the tongues of three wagons with neck yokes and ran a lariat through each of the loops at the end of the tongue. The rustlers were hanged, and their bodies taken down and buried.

Another time, a number of cowboys found some of their cattle in a little pasture that had been fenced by a homesteader who lived nearby in a dugout. The cowboys went to the dugout that night and called the homesteader out. When accused of rustling the cattle, he asserted his innocence. It did no good. While the homesteader's wife pleaded for her husband, he was taken by the cowboys to an elm tree on a nearby creek and hanged. As the cowboys were returning to their headquarters, they met the real rustler putting another bunch of cattle in the little pasture of the man whom they had just hanged. They promptly hanged the real rustler, then went back to the dugout of the homesteader, where the widow thought they were coming for her. She pleaded with them for her life, but they only laughed as they told her they had hanged the wrong man, her husband.

Most of the settlers and cattlemen in the strip were good people who respected the rights of others, but the unique nature of the strip attracted outlaws, gamblers, saloon keepers, and what one early set- tler, Elmer E. Brown, called "the scum of civilization." The vigilante committees had their hands full, especially after some residents de- cided to profit from jumping land claims and from "road trotting" A road trotter would suddenly appear at a settler's dugout claiming that he had made a previous claim on that spot. He would then tell the settler that he would relinquish his claim for a sum of money. The settler would have to pay up in order to hold his claim or else leave.

Claim jumpers were another breed. Indiana native Olive M. Nelson, who took up a claim in 1887 near modern Bison, Oklahoma, related how two men in Beaver, Charley Tracy, who ran a feed barn and livery stable, and a man named Bennett, who ran a grocery store, decided to make easy money by hiring another man, Thompson, to jump a land claim, sell out, and then divide the money among the three of them.

Vigilantes soon learned what the three men were doing and went after them. They first caught Thompson, beat him up, and later shot him twenty-four times. Next they found and killed Bennett. They then went looking for Charley Tracy, who had heard the sound of shooting and had decided to leave town. He harnessed two ponies and hooked them to a buggy in which his wife was already sitting. When the vigilantes came into sight, Tracy lashed the ponies, and the buggy left Beaver at full speed. Tracy headed for Meade Center, Kan-

A settler's family posing in front of their Oklahoma Panhandle sod house and windmill after law and order came to the region. (Courtesy Western History Collections, University of Oklahoma Library)

sas, several miles north. There he persuaded the town marshal to put him in jail for a few days of protection. Tracy never returned to the strip.

After that incident, claim jumping around Beaver was never very popular. Meanwhile, citizens had been working to organize the strip as Cimarron Territory. On February 22, 1887, the first territorial election was held. Nine delegates were chosen. The following month, a territorial council was created at Beaver, the projected capital of Cimarron Territory. They divided the strip into five counties, made laws, and decided to send a delegate to Washington, D.C., to seek congressional recognition of Cimarron Territory.

They elected Dr. Owen G. Chase to go to Washington. But another political faction in the strip was led by J. E. Dale. They argued over purely local issues, but the group sent Dale to Washington to be the delegate. Either Chase or Dale probably would have been seated if it had not been for the opposition of the other. Congress gave some attention to the proposal to establish Cimarron Territory, but in the end, they realized that the planned territory was not large enough in population and resources to justify creation as a territory. The possibility of a state of Cimarron was dead.

When the New York *Sun* printed a sensational story about the strip being a refuge for outlaws and riffraff, the story gave the strip the label "No-Man's-Land." No longer did people refer to it as "the strip." The land that was larger than the states of Rhode Island and Delaware became known as "No-Man's-Land."

The foundation for law and order and other elements of civilization came in May 1890, when No-Man's-Land became part of the new Territory of Oklahoma. By then, however, the strip had lost population. Perhaps two-thirds of its residents left in the summer of 1889 to participate in the land run of April 22, 1889. When Oklahoma became a state on November 16, 1907, No-Man's-Land became the Oklahoma Panhandle and was divided into the three counties that exist today: Beaver, Texas, and Cimarron.

18

The Prizefight Texas Didn't Want

It was early December 1895 when promoter Dan Stuart, a portly little man from East Texas, smiled to himself as he reread a telegram he had just received. It read, "Accept offer. Stop. Wire location. Signed, Peter Maher."

Stuart had promoted just about everything from circuses to prizefights. He first got Bob Fitzsimmons, the world's middleweight champion, to agree to fight Maher, the Irish champion. Now, the telegram confirmed that Maher had agreed to the match. Stuart could now arrange the boxing match, but he had a problem. The manly sport was taking a beating from California to New York. Laws banning prizefighting were being enacted just about everywhere. Stuart did not know where he could hold the fight.

Only four months earlier, Stuart had scheduled a match in Dallas between Gentlemen Jim Corbett and Bob Fitzsimmons. At the time, Texas was one of the few states without an antiprizefighting law. Governor Charles Culberson, however, found prizefighting disgusting and resented Dan Stuart, an old political foe. Culberson called a special session of the Texas legislature, and on October 3, 1895, that body made prizefighting illegal in Texas, "punishable by confinement in the state penitentiary." Governor Culberson vowed that so long as he was in office, Texas would not become a prizefighting commonwealth.

Dan Stuart then arranged to hold the fight in Arkansas, but Corbett and Fitzsimmons were arrested as they crossed the state line. Both were charged with conspiracy to assault the other. Gentleman Jim quickly cooled to prizefighting, choosing a calmer life of making theatrical appearances. At Stuart's urging, Gentleman Jim announced that he would step down as champion in favor of the winner of a proposed bout between Peter Maher and another fighter named O'Donnell. The Maher-O'Donnell fight was held in Nevada and Maher won, which was just what Stuart wanted because it laid the foundation for what he believed was the "fight of the century."

Fight fans had been calling for a rematch of Fitzsimmons. With Maher now holding Corbett's title, the promotional possibilities were great. Fitzsimmons, who had beaten Maher before, was first to tell Stuart he would fight. Then Maher, wanting a chance to reverse his previous defeat and boost his standing, wired Stuart that he would fight Fitzsimmons. Now it was up to Stuart to find a place to hold the fight.

The major sporting towns across America had antiprizefight laws. The few towns that did not were too small to support such a fight. Stuart put out the word that Fitzsimmons and Maher had agreed to fight and that he was looking for a site. To his surprise, a group of sporting businessmen in El Paso, Texas, offered him $6,000 to bring the bout there. They also offered a purse of $10,000 for the winner of the fight.

Stuart had not expected an offer from Texas because it had a new antiprizefighting law. He knew El Paso had never been much of a sporting town, but he also knew El Paso was a wide-open town and pretty isolated from the rest of Texas. Its location might be perfect. Stuart knew if he could not hold the fight in El Paso, he could easily move it across the Rio Grande into Old Mexico, or into New Mexico Territory, only a few miles away. Or he could move it farther west to Arizona, a quick overnight train trip west.

Promoter Stuart accepted the El Paso offer and set the fight date as February 14, 1896, Valentine's Day. When the word reached El Paso, the town went wild. Businessmen started making plans for what they hoped would be a mammoth invasion of free-spending fight fans. Just after Christmas 1895, fight fans began arriving in El Paso, along with pickpockets, prostitutes, and gamblers, all of whom wanted to cash in on the fight. Bob Fitzsimmons arrived in late December and set up his training camp in Juarez, just across the Rio Grande in Old Mexico. Two weeks later, in early January 1896, Peter Maher arrived by train and set up his camp at Las Cruces in New Mexico Territory, about forty miles northwest of El Paso. Stuart's secretary, W. K. Wheelock, arrived in El Paso and established headquarters in the Sheldon Block of the city.

Excitement began to build, and fans arrived to watch Fitzsimmons and Maher train. Preachers opposed to prizefighting also arrived at the "Paris of Texas," as one eastern newspaper described El Paso, and set up shop at the First Methodist Church. They competed against the gamblers and other undesirables who wanted to get everything they could from any unsuspecting residents or visitors.

On February 9, 1896, five days before the announced date of the fight, Dan Stuart himself arrived by train. Glowing with confidence, he expounded on the glories of boxing and what a radiant future the manly sport of kings had. "Nothing short of lightning or the destruction of the earth by fire or flood can stop the contests we have arranged to pull off. It's a cold 200 to 1 shot that they'll come off as advertised," Stuart told reporters, who had come from all over the nation.

Stuart was so confident that he announced that an even greater event, a "Fistic Carnival," a week-long celebration beginning after the "fight of the century" would be held. It would include four other boxing matches, "three of them for world championships." Stuart said an arena would be built to house more than 20,000 people, and "seats will cost from ten to forty dollars each."

During the mornings of the carnival, Stuart said audiences would be able to watch six famous Spanish bullfighters who would be arriving from Madrid. The prizefights would be held in the afternoons. Stuart said that during the week, there also would be a "cowboy tournament," or rodeo, held just outside of El Paso. Businessmen, gamblers, pickpockets, prostitutes, and other visitors to El Paso were overjoyed with the news.

When word of Stuart's plans reached Austin, about five hundred miles to the east, Governor Culberson ordered W. H. Mabry, the Texas adjutant general, to take the Texas rangers and stop any attempt to hold prizefights in El Paso. Mabry sent Captain John Hughes and his company of rangers to El Paso. They arrived and set up camp near El Paso.

When Stuart learned this, the promoter appeared to be cool and calm. He told reporters, "No combination that does not involve the death of the principals can prevent the meeting of the men matched." Then, in an apparent effort to scare off the rangers, Stuart spread a rumor that Bat Masterson was coming to El Paso with a hundred fighting men to see that the fight would come off on schedule. Masterson came, but alone, and not to help Stuart. Like hundreds of other visitors, Masterson came to see the "fight of the century."

Meanwhile, the presence of the rangers brought law and order to El Paso—at least on the surface. The rangers began to cramp the style of the undesirables, who had been doing almost anything they wanted. Some of the crooks and hoodlums claimed El Paso had been placed under martial law and that their freedom and liberty had been violated. The rangers ignored their claims.

Stuart appeared undaunted by the rangers' presence, but he quickly and quietly persuaded the El Paso city council to meet and denounce Governor Culberson for ordering the rangers to El Paso, Texas Adjutant General Mabry for sending them, and the rangers for coming. The city council's action, however, was immediately opposed by the El Paso Minister's Union, which represented the town's more law-abiding citizens. The ministers began openly attacking prize-fighting as brutal and indecent.

Stuart ignored them, but he soon asked W. K. Wheelock, his secretary, to answer the charges. Wheelock responded by saying the ministers misunderstood modern boxing—that it had changed considerably since the mid-1870s: "The Marquis of Queensberry's rules require that five-ounce gloves be used, and this fact, along with certain rules, has taken the brutality out of the affair," said Wheelock, who added that boxing had become a refined sport that is witnessed "by the most refined people."

Unshaken by Wheelock's comments, the ministers continued their attack on boxing from their pulpits, through newspapers, and in eloquent appeals. Texas Governor Culberson assured the ministers he would not let the fights be held on Texas soil. It was then that the governor of Chihuahua, just across the border in Mexico, ordered a hundred fifty cavalrymen to the border, saying he did not want the prizefights moved to Mexico.

The ministers feared that Stuart might move the fights to New Mexico Territory. They appealed to William T. Thornton, the territorial governor, but he replied that he was powerless to prevent any prizefights there, although he personally disliked boxing. Hearing what Thornton had said, the ministers sent telegrams to congressmen in Washington, D.C., advising them that the fights would undoubtedly be held in New Mexico Territory, and neither territorial law nor federal law prohibited such fights. Could not Congress prohibit them?

Congress could—and did. New Mexico's territorial delegate, Tom Catron, quickly got a bill passed making it a felony to hold a prizefight for money in any territory of the United States. This included Arizona Territory, an optional site that Stuart had considered. The ministers cheered, but Stuart did not waver. He told reporters in El Paso, "No power in heaven or on earth can stop the fights unless a national calamity intervenes."

Fearing serious trouble, Texas Adjutant General Mabry left Austin for El Paso, taking with him two ranger captains, John H. Rogers and J. B. Brooks, plus an additional ten rangers. When Mabry reached El Paso, he told reporters that ranger Captain Bill McDonald, then one of the best-known rangers in Texas, was on his way to El Paso from Amarillo to help. Mabry declared that nearly every ranger in Texas would be in El Paso "to make certain there is no violation of the anti–prize-fight law." Any other promoter probably would have given up at this point, but not Stuart. He told a growing number of reporters, "The fight will be held, and I will not violate Texas law."

It was now the evening of February 13, 1896, the night before the fight was scheduled. Stuart was under tremendous pressure to tell people where the fight would be held. At 8 P.M., Stuart announced, "Come around to headquarters tomorrow and the location of the fight will be announced." The following morning, however, Stuart announced that the fight had been postponed, although not because the locale was in question: "The Irish Champ, Maher, came down from Las Cruces this morning with badly inflamed eyes. He has acute epithelioma. The fight will be delayed one week."

Fitzsimmons did not like this. He demanded that Maher forfeit his appearance money of $1,000, but Stuart quickly calmed Fitzsimmons down by telling him that "the fight will definitely take place on Friday, February 21." Fitzsimmons agreed to wait. Stuart then announced that the lesser fights had been called off because of Maher's eye condition, and that the Fistic Carnival was canceled. Stuart assured everyone that "the fight of the century" would be held. The news of the delay sent many fight fans packing. They had either gone broke waiting or were fed up paying exorbitant prices for food and lodging.

Meanwhile, Texas ranger Captain Bill McDonald arrived in El Paso. He, along with Texas Adjutant General Mabry and fellow ranger Captains Brooks, Hughes, and Rogers, met and decided to locate the physician who supposedly had treated Maher's eyes. The rangers located a Dr. Yandell, but he told them he had never even seen Maher, much less diagnosed his condition. It was obvious to Mabry and the rangers that Stuart had concocted the story about Maher's eye trouble as a delaying tactic to provide more time to find a place to hold the fight.

Mabry immediately assigned two groups of three rangers each to follow Maher and Fitzsimmons. Mabry ordered three other rangers, including McDonald, to follow Stuart. Blue-eyed and soft-spoken, McDonald was best equipped of all the rangers to handle Stuart. McDonald had the ability to stage himself before those he dealt with capitalizing on the ranger tradition of courage and a job well done. Mabry, not taking any chances, also detailed three other rangers, including Edwin Aten, who already was assigned guard service on the Southern Pacific line between El Paso and Del Rio, to watch for shipments of the lumber for the ring and other paraphernalia for the fight, figuring that where it went, the fight was sure to go.

Stuart kept quiet and remained out of public view. As everyone waited, speculation grew. One rumor surfaced that claimed the fight would be held in the mountains near El Paso, in an area that only could be reached through a narrow pass that could easily be defended. Another rumor said the fighters would secretly leave El Paso by train and go to Galveston on the Texas coast, where a barge would be towed into the Gulf of Mexico and the fight held many miles offshore. In truth, no one, not even Stuart, knew what was going to happen.

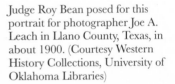

Judge Roy Bean posed for this portrait for photographer Joe A. Leach in Llano County, Texas, in about 1900. (Courtesy Western History Collections, University of Oklahoma Libraries)

Nearly four hundred miles southeast of El Paso at Langtry, Texas, Judge Roy Bean, a bearded saloon keeper and justice of the peace, had been following Stuart's problem. Bean sent Stuart a telegram inviting him to bring the fight to Langtry, and he assured Stuart that because he was the "Law West of the Pecos," he would see that there was no interference. Stuart immediately accepted Bean's invitation but kept it a secret.

To Stuart, Langtry seemed like the perfect paradise for pugilism. It was located in an unsettled, desolate part of southwest Texas where only railroad workers, gamblers, rustlers, and thieves congregated. The fact that the Southern Pacific Railway ran between El Paso and Langtry provided fast transportation for the fighters, fans, and Stuart.

On February 20, 1896, one day before the fight was scheduled, ranger Edwin Aten observed the lumber for the fight ring being loaded on a flatcar and hooked up to a westbound freight train. As the train pulled out, the ranger climbed aboard and rode to Strauss, just across the border in New Mexico Territory. It was a trick by Stuart to make the rangers believe that the fight was going to be held in

New Mexico. Aten stayed with the flatcar carrying the lumber and equipment, which was then brought back through El Paso on a southeast-bound train. Four hundred miles later, ranger Aten found himself in Langtry, watching carpenters unload the flatcar and hurriedly begin building the fight ring. The ranger sent a telegram to Mabry explaining what had happened.

About 5 P.M. that afternoon in El Paso, promoter Stuart posted a notice on the window of his El Paso headquarters. It read, "Persons desirous of attending the prizefight will report at these headquarters tonight at 9:45 o'clock. Railroad fare for the round trip will not exceed $12.00." As people gathered at Stuart's headquarters, he announced that the fight would take place in Langtry. Less than two hours later, Stuart, the fighters, fans, and about half of the Texas rangers in El Paso boarded a hastily expanded eastbound train and headed for Langtry.

The trip was uneventful until early in the morning, when the train stopped at the small Texas town of Sanderson, a little more than halfway to Langtry. Everyone aboard was tired and hungry. Many of the passengers, including Stuart, Mabry, Bat Masterson, and ranger Captain McDonald, hurried to a nearby Chinese restaurant. The Chinese waiters scurried about doing their best to serve the customers. Masterson, however, thought one waiter was not moving fast enough. Masterson stopped the waiter and gave him a talking to. When the waiter replied that he was doing his best, Masterson picked up a large table caster and started to swing it toward the waiter.

Ranger Captain McDonald, sitting nearby, jumped to his feet, grabbed Masterson's arm, and told him not to hit the waiter. Masterson wheeled on McDonald and growled that maybe McDonald would like to take it up. "I done took it up," was McDonald's only reply, which he made while staring right into Masterson's eyes. A moment later, Masterson put the caster down. Both men sat down at their tables and finished their meals.

It was cloudy and a cold drizzle fell when the train arrived in Langtry at about 3 P.M. on February 21. Another special train from the east, carrying more fight fans, had arrived earlier. As Stuart got off his train, Mabry warned Stuart that the fight could not be held in Texas. Judge Roy Bean, standing nearby, walked up and said the fight

Judge Roy Bean, the "Law West of the Pecos," is holding court on the front porch of his Jersey Lilly saloon in Langtry, Texas, in 1900. (Courtesy Western History Collections, University of Oklahoma Libraries)

wouldn't be held on Texas soil. Bean told Mabry the bout would take place on a sandbar in the Rio Grande.

"No, that's still Texas soil," replied Mabry.

Judge Bean disagreed and hurriedly held court in his saloon, the Jersey Lilly, ruling that the sandbar was in Mexico, not Texas, probably knowing that Mexican authorities would not have time to send troops to stop the fight. Mabry and the rangers said nothing. They went along with Bean. He was an officer of the court, a justice of the peace. The irony of it was that only a few years earlier, the rangers had gotten Bean appointed to the job because they needed a court in that part of Texas where lawbreakers could be tried. Bean had been the only person willing to take the job.

As soon as Bean's court closed, he reopened the bar on the other side of the room and sold beer at a dollar a bottle. Warmed by the spirits, the fans began filing outside into the drizzle, then followed a rocky path down through a canyon to the banks of the Rio Grande. There a temporary bridge had been constructed from the Texas side of the river to a large sandbar in the middle of the Rio Grande. That

The temporary bridge constructed from the United States side of the Rio Grande to a large sandbar in the river where the fight was held. Fight fans used the bridge to reach the fight ring. (Courtesy Western History Collections, University of Oklahoma Libraries)

sandbar, according to Judge Bean's ruling, was in the Mexican state of Coahuila and therefore was out of reach of Texas law, and the rangers.

Around a hastily built boxing ring was a canvas wall to keep the nonpaying fight fans from seeing the bout. The rangers, however, did not follow the fans to the fight ring. With other nonpaying spectators, the rangers sat on the rocky rim of the canyon perhaps two hundred feet above the ring. Although they were some distance away, they had a good view of the ring.

At 4:15 P.M., with drizzle still falling, a confident Bob Fitzsimmons climbed through the ropes, followed by a somewhat paler Maher. Fitzsimmon's manager asked referee George Siler if the prize money was at ringside. Siler produced two certified checks. Fitzsimmon's manger demanded, "I want money. Those checks are no good to us," but Fitzsimmons then said, "I'm going to fight to satisfy the public, money or no money, but this will be the last time I will ever give under."

The boxing ring constructed on a large sandbar in the Rio Grande. The canvas fence was built to keep nonpaying fight fans from seeing the bout. (Courtesy Western History Collections, University of Oklahoma Libraries)

The crowd cheered as the drizzle continued to fall.

Then, without any preliminary sparring, the fight began. Fitzsimmons and Maher exchanged blows. Maher pushed Fitzsimmons to the ropes in a clinch, then broke in the center of the ring. A moment later, Fitzsimmons hooked Maher's jaw with his right glove. Maher fell backward to the canvas like a lead balloon. The "fight of the century" was over. It had lasted one minute and thirty-five seconds. When he recovered, Maher said, "I thought I had him licked until he pushed me under the jaw and then it was all over with me and I quit thinking."

Watching from the canyon rim, some of the rangers smiled at the outcome. Others were half-disgusted. All were happy that the fight was over and that officially, at least according to Judge Roy Bean, it had not been fought on Texas soil. As for promoter Dan Stuart, he seemed satisfied that with the help of Judge Bean, he had pulled off the fight without interference and had technically not violated Texas law. But for the rest of the spectators, the whole thing seemed anticlimactic as Stuart, the fighters, and their parties, along with the fans, crossed the bridge over the Rio Grande and climbed the bank, heading for the Jersey Lilly to warm their damp bones.

19

Who Murdered Belle Starr?

She was shot in the back; four buckshot took effect, three in the center of the neck and one in the back. She was knocked from her horse and her slayer climbed the fence and shot her a second time with a heavy charge of turkey shot as she lay on her back in the mud, the charge taking effect in the face, neck and one arm. Belle spoke one or two words, gasped and died. Neighbors gathered and the body was carried to the mountain home, a mile away.

This description of the murder of outlaw Belle Starr was written by Samuel W. Harman and included in his exceedingly rare book *Hell on the Border*, published in Fort Smith, Arkansas, in 1898.

Whether Harman's details of Belle Starr's violent death are factual is not known. It may have been based on dime novels or sensational newspaper accounts that undoubtedly enhanced the legend of Belle Starr. There is no question that she was an extraordinary woman, perhaps in the class of Calamity Jane and Cattle Kate Watson. As Harman notes in his book, "there is something awful to contemplate in the thought of a woman dying 'with her boots on.'"

Belle Starr was born Myra Belle Shirley on a rolling prairie farm near Carthage, Missouri, in 1848. Border troubles during the late 1850s forced her family to move to Texas, where, in 1866, Belle met Cole Younger, of the infamous Younger brothers. He may have fa-

Apparently believing everything
written about her, Belle Starr
posed with her revolvers for a
photographer, perhaps in Fort
Smith, Arkansas, during the
1880s. (Courtesy Western History
Collections, University of
Oklahoma Libraries)

thered her first child. The romance, however, was short-lived. She
soon took up with another outlaw, Jim Reed, and journeyed to California. There Belle gave Reed a son.

In 1869, Belle and Jim returned to Texas, where they made their
living robbing and rustling cattle in the area around Dallas. Dressed
in velvet skirts and plumed hats and riding her mare, Venus, Belle
became known as the "Bandit Queen."

Tragedy struck in 1874 when Belle's husband was killed by a
member of his own gang. Belle left her children with her mother and
traveled north into Indian Territory, into what is now eastern Oklahoma. There, in the Sans Bois Mountains, she led her own gang of
cattle rustlers and horse thieves and eventually began living with a
Cherokee Indian named Sam Starr.

The law caught up with Sam and Belle. Both were indicted on
a charge of horse stealing. Belle has the dubious honor of being the
first woman ever tried for a major crime in "Hanging Judge" Isaac

Belle Starr, on her famous horse. She is America's most noted female bandit, the gamest, who ever rode a range, and she is also the first white woman to locate in Oklahoma Territory.

This photograph of Belle Starr mounted on her horse was taken by Fort Smith, Arkansas, photographers in 1887, about two years before her death. (Courtesy Western History Collections, University of Oklahoma Libraries)

Parker's Arkansas court at Fort Smith. After five months in federal prison in Detroit, Belle and Sam returned to Indian Territory and resumed their dishonorable profession.

Tragedy struck again in 1886. Sam Starr was killed in a gunfight. Belle wasted no time and soon took up with a young Creek Indian named Jim July. Unfortunately, Belle's history seemed to repeat itself. Within two years, the law caught up with Jim, and he was taken to Fort Smith to face larceny charges.

Belle Starr decided to go part of the way with Jim but turned back before reaching Fort Smith. While on her way home, she was shot and killed. That was on February 3, 1889. It was her forty-third birthday.

Some people thought Jim July killed her. Others said she was murdered by her enraged son, Ed Reed. Still others said it was a man named E. A. Watson, a man Belle reportedly had threatened to turn into the law for a murder he had committed. Even the name Jim Middleton, brother of a former lover, was mentioned. But no one was ever convicted for the murder, and for decades the speculation has continued.

In the summer of 1970, another name was added to the list. LeRoy Towns, then editor of *Midway,* the Sunday magazine of the *Topeka Capital-Journal,* was working at his desk when a man asked to see him. The visitor was A. J. Robinson, then seventy-two years old, of Topeka, Kansas. He said he had a story to tell. Towns listened.

Robinson said he had gone to visit his grandmother in Oklahoma in 1911 or 1912. At the time he was about twelve years old.

"We went one day to visit my grandmother. I think it was Sunday morning or afternoon. We were just sitting around talking and she was telling us about the hard times she had had in Indian Territory," he said. "Then her face lit up and she said, 'I've got something to tell all of you. . . . I killed Belle Starr.'"

Robinson told Towns he decided to tell the story because he was the only person alive who then knew it, and he didn't want the story lost. Robinson added that his grandmother swore all those present to secrecy—Robinson, his mother and father, and an aunt name Lucinda.

Why secrecy? Robinson said it may have been because of the family reputation or because early in the twentieth century, revenge by one of the infamous Younger gang might have been possible. He wasn't sure.

Regardless, Robinson then related that his grandmother was named Nana, perhaps Nannie, Devena. At the time he heard her story, she was a middle-aged widow who weighed about ninety-five pounds. Her skin was dark and leathery, the result of much outdoor living, and she was fond of smoking wood chips in a crusty corncob pipe.

Robinson said Mrs. Devena was born in the 1840s in South Carolina. He did not know her maiden name. She was proud of her French blood. Sometime before 1880, she and her husband moved west to Indian Territory and set up housekeeping on the Canadian River near Eufaula, in what is now eastern Oklahoma. By 1889, there were five children—one being Rene—and Mrs. Devena, then in her thirties, was a widow.

Belle Starr, he added, was her neighbor.

The events leading to Belle Starr's death, according to Robinson, began when "Grandmother sent her boys over to hoe cotton for a neighbor named Jim. The family needed the money. But other neighbors—I don't recall their name—didn't like Jim, and so they didn't like the kids helping him in the field."

The neighbors, said Robinson, first warned Mrs. Devena not to let her sons hoe Jim's cotton. She glowered, gritted her teeth, and told them to go to hell. But then one night, Mrs. Devena's milk cows were turned loose.

"She would hear them being turned out, and would go down to put them back in," said Robinson, adding, "That went on for several nights." Once, he said, "she caught her villainous neighbors stealing corn from her crib. She set a bear trap and returned the next morning to find one of the neighbor boys caught and in pain."

The feud grew hotter with the passing of weeks. The neighbors put out stronger warnings, hinting "something might happen if you don't stop being friendly with Jim."

One night it did.

As Mrs. Devena went to the corral, she was struck, thrown to the ground, and beaten. Her screams brought a daughter from the house, but not before Mrs. Devena recognized her attacker as one of the neighbor boys.

"As she told us that day," recalled Robinson, "she went back up to the house, took down the old muzzle-loader from its hook and loaded it. Then she went down to the road and waited."

Mrs. Devena saw her attacker trot off to the nearby town on horseback. She then hunkered down at the side of the rode to wait his return. How long she waited is not recorded, but later she saw a horse and rider coming from the direction of town. She strained to make out the rider in the growing darkness. The rider was wearing a wide-brimmed hat. Certainly, it must be the guilty neighbor. A few yards closer, and she pulled the trigger.

"A little while after that they found Belle dead at the exact spot she [Mrs. Devena] shot the rider out of the saddle," said Robinson.

That was the story told by A. J. Robinson in 1970.

Is it true?

It seems possible that in the darkness, Mrs. Devena might have killed Belle Starr by mistake. Belle Starr did wear hats like men, and in the growing darkness, her silhouette could have been mistaken for that of a young man—the neighbor boy she undoubtedly intended to kill.

And what about "Jim," the man for whom Mrs. Devena's sons hoed cotton? Was he Jim July, Belle's lover?

These and many other questions remain unanswered. Robinson's story has simply added one more name to the list of people who might have killed Belle Starr. Today, her remains still lie buried in a wooden casket in a grave at Eufaula, Oklahoma. As for Mrs. Devena, she died in the 1930s and was buried in Sand Springs, Oklahoma. At her death, she was nearly one hundred years old.

20

Who Was Seth Bullock?

Dime novels of the late nineteenth and early twentieth centuries were cheap, easy to obtain, and provided escape for eastern working-class readers trapped in big-city slums. They made the West seem romantic. They were similar to the Hollywood Western movies produced from the 1820s into the 1950s and more recent Westerns on television. Their purpose was to entertain.

Although some events in Seth Bullock's life were incorporated in a few dime novels, he was never identified by his full name and therefore never attained the legendary status of Buffalo Bill, James B. "Wild Bill" Hickok, and other real-life characters whose stories were embellished in dime novels. It was not until the twenty-first century that the name "Seth Bullock" gained notoriety as a principal character in the HBO television series *Deadwood.* Even then, Bullock's full story was not told.

Seth Bullock was a real man who made a name for himself as a lawman, politician, entrepreneur, soldier, and friend of Teddy Roosevelt. The facts of his life alone are colorful without embellishment. Born in Amherstburg, Ontario, Canada, July 23, 1849, his father was George Bullock, a retired British major, and his mother was Agnes Findley Bullock, of Scottish ancestry.

When Seth was five, the family was living in Sandwich, Ontario, where his father entered local politics. Seth was undoubtedly influ-

Seth Bullock (left) and Teddy Roosevelt. This photo was taken early in the twentieth century. Roosevelt first met Bullock on the cattle range in 1884. They became very good friends. Roosevelt appointed Bullock U.S. marshal for South Dakota soon after he became president. (Author's Collection)

enced by his father's involvement in politics and community affairs, but he soon came to resent his father's strict military-style discipline. When Seth was sixteen, he ran away from home and lived a short time with a grown sister in Montana until she sent him home.

Seth remained at home until he was eighteen, when he again left and returned to Montana. In 1867, he was in Helena, where he ran unsuccessfully for the territorial legislature. Later, he tried again and was elected to the territorial senate. He served in 1871 and 1872. As a senator, young Bullock, who was about twenty-two, introduced a resolution memorializing Congress to set aside land in northwest Wyoming for a great national park. The Montana territorial legislature adopted the resolution and sent it to Washington, D.C. Later a bill was introduced in both houses of Congress, and Yellowstone National Park was established by federal statute on March 1, 1872.

In 1874, Seth married his childhood sweetheart, Marguerite "Martha" Eccles, a school teacher from Tecumseh, Michigan, in a ceremony at Salt Lake City. He then took his bride to Helena, where he was a deputy sheriff. A year later, he was elected sheriff of Lewis and Clark County. Seth was well known in the community as an auctioneer and chief engineer of the Helena fire department, and he had an imposing appearance that commanded instant respect. He was a tall man who stood erect, and his steely gray eyes beneath his bushy eyebrows were piercing. He looked like a lawman.

Seth became partners with Solomon "Sol" Star and opened a hardware business in Helena. Star, a native of Bavaria and nine years older than Bullock, came to America in about 1850. He first settled in Ohio, where he clerked in a general store in 1857. When the Civil War began, he took some merchandise to Missouri and went into business. When the war ended, he headed for the Montana mining town of Virginia City with more merchandise and opened a store that he operated until 1872. Star was then appointed receiver of the land office in Helena, where Star and Seth Bullock became good friends and business partners.

When news reached Helena in 1876 of a gold discovery in the Black Hills of modern South Dakota, Seth sent his wife to Michigan and the safety of her parents' home. He did so because he and Star saw a business opportunity in the new and rough mining town of Deadwood. They knew the gold seekers would need tools.

By August 1876, they were in the mining town of Deadwood, where they purchased a lot and set up their business, first in a tent and later in a building. The day after Bullock arrived in Deadwood, "Wild Bill" Hickok was shot in the back and killed by Jack McCall. The shooting was the straw that broke the camel's back. The people of Deadwood wanted the lawlessness to end. When responsible townspeople learned of Bullock's reputation as a lawman in Montana, they made him sheriff.

Sheriff Bullock hired a few good deputies and began to clean up Deadwood, bringing stability to the mining town. Bullock's main problem was Al Swearengen, who had arrived in the mining town a

Deadwood as photographed by F. Jay Haynes in 1877, about a year after Seth
Bullock arrived. (Courtesy The Haynes Foundation)

few months before Bullock. Swearengen opened the Gem Theatre, a
dance hall that was really a brothel. Swearengen, who had formed
alliances with a few prominent and powerful men in Deadwood, became off limits for Sheriff Bullock.

Deadwood, however, was peaceful enough for Bullock to send
for his wife, Martha, and their daughter, Margaret. In time, the Bullocks would have another daughter, Florence, and a son, Stanley.
Seth's business partner, Sol Star, never married, but the two men soon
purchased a ranch where the Redwater Creek meets the Belle Fourche
River and formed the S&B Ranch Company to expand their business
interests.

In 1884, Bullock became a deputy U.S. marshal in eastern Da-
kota Territory. That year he was bringing in a horse thief known as
"Crazy Steve" when Bullock met a deputy sheriff from what is now
Medora, North Dakota. The deputy was none other than Theodore
Roosevelt, future president of the United States. Later, Roosevelt
wrote in his autobiography:

I went down to Deadwood on business, Sylvane Ferris and I on horseback, while Bill Jones drove the wagon. At a little town, Spearfish, I think, after crossing the last eighty or ninety miles of gumbo prairie, we met Seth Bullock. We had had rather a rough trip, and had lain out for a fortnight, so I suppose we looked somewhat unkempt. Seth received us with rather distant courtesy at first, but unbent when he found out who we were, remarking, "You see, by your looks I thought you were some kind of a tin-horn gambling outfit, and that I might have to keep an eye on you!" He then inquired after the capture of "Steve"—with a little of the air of one sportsman when another has shot a quail that either might have claimed—"My bird, I believe?" Later Seth Bullock became, and has ever since remained, one of my staunchest and most valued friends.

Bullock first met Roosevelt near what became the town of Belle Fourche in 1890, one year after South Dakota became a state. Bullock and Sol Star gave the Fremont, Elkhorn, and Missouri Valley Railroad forty acres of free land on their S&B Ranch for the line's right of way. It was on this route that Bullock and Star established the town of Belle Fourche, which later became the largest livestock shipping point in the United States.

In Deadwood, fire destroyed the Bullock and Star hardware store in 1894. Rather than rebuild, the two men built a three-story luxury hotel on the site. The Bullock Hotel, as it was called, was Italianate in style, with a banded façade of local white and pink sandstone. It had sixty-four rooms, steam heat, and indoor bathrooms on each floor.

During the Spanish-American War, Bullock volunteered for service in the cavalry and became a captain in Troop A of Grigsby's Cowboy Regiment. But the unit never saw combat. Unit members spent most of their time at Camp Thomas in Georgia before being mustered out in September 1898.

Sol Star died in 1891, and his funeral reportedly would have been fit for royalty. Bullock maintained correspondence with Teddy Roosevelt, whose teenage sons spent their summer vacations with Seth Bullock, tasting western life.

When William McKinley became president in 1897 and Roosevelt vice president, Bullock was appointed the first forest supervisor of the Black Hills Reserve. After President McKinley was shot in Buffalo, New York, and died September 14, 1901, Roosevelt, not quite forty-three, became president; he completed McKinley's term and was elected president in his own right. Bullock organized fifty riders, including Hollywood Western star Tom Mix, to ride in the inaugural parade in 1905.

Roosevelt soon appointed Bullock the U.S. marshal for South Dakota. Bullock was reappointed in 1909 by President William Howard Taft and continued in office for a year under President Woodrow Wilson.

After Roosevelt's term as president ended in 1909, he went to Africa and then to London. As Roosevelt later wrote in his autobiography, "On getting back to Europe I cabled Seth Bullock to bring over Mrs. Bullock and meet me in London, which he did; by that time I felt that I just had to meet my own people, who spoke my neighborhood dialect." The Roosevelts and the Bullocks had a grand time.

Nine years later, when President Roosevelt died on January 6, 1919, in Oyster Bay, New York, Bullock was not in good health. He was determined, however, to create a monument to Roosevelt in South Dakota. With help from the Society of Black Hills Pioneers, Bullock had a tower constructed of Black Hills stone erected on the crest of Sheep Mountain north of Deadwood. A plaque on the tower includes the pioneer society's resolution renaming the peak Mount Roosevelt. It was dedicated July 4, 1919, the first memorial to Theodore Roosevelt in the United States.

Bullock's efforts to pay tribute to his beloved friend taxed his will. Two months later, in September 1919, Seth Bullock died at the age of seventy in room 211 of the Bullock Hotel in Deadwood. He was buried in Mount Moriah cemetery at Deadwood. From his grave, visitors can see Mount Roosevelt in the distance.

21

The Law and
Cattle Town Gamblers

Across the plains and prairies, Indians had gambled on games, foot-races, and horse races long before the first white man arrived. Even after the early white settlers arrived, gambling was not perceived as a moral issue until Texans began driving herds of longhorns north to the Kansas railheads.

Almost instinctively, gamblers knew that lots of money would change hands in the cattle towns. Cattle buyers would buy longhorns from the Texans, and the cowboys who drove the cattle north would be paid for their work. Cattle towns were exactly what gamblers looked for: a place where they could take hard-earned dollars away from trail-weary cowboys.

Abilene was the first Kansas cattle town located on the Eastern Division of the Union Pacific railway, later the Kansas Pacific. There also was Ellsworth, to the west of Abilene on the same line, which was a cattle town from 1871 until fall 1875. On the newly built Atchison, Topeka, and Santa Fe line, Newton was a short-lived cattle town in 1871. The following year, the trade shifted to Wichita, where the trade remained until fall 1876. The trade then moved west to Dodge City, a town that enjoyed the cattle trade through 1885. Gamblers plied their trade in each of these cattle towns.

Front Street in Dodge City, Kansas, in the late 1870s, soon after the cattle trade arrived along with gamblers. Front Street faced the railroad tracks of the Atchison, Topeka, and Santa Fe railroad. (Courtesy Western History Collections, University of Oklahoma Libraries)

New cattle towns appeared each time the legislature moved the quarantine line farther west of where homesteaders and settlers were building their homes. The quarantine line marked the line of westward settlement in Kansas. East of that line, longhorns were prohibited from being driven overland because they were thought to carry Texas fever, which killed domestic cattle. (Texas fever actually came from a tick on the longhorns, but this was not discovered until several years later.)

When Abilene ceased being a cattle town in 1871, the gamblers left. Gamblers followed the cattle cycle: they left the cattle town each fall, only to return in the spring to whatever cattle town seemed best. The prostitutes followed the same pattern. Of course, both groups made certain the cattle town they chose each season had plenty of saloons where they could ply their trade.

Professional people in Abilene were the first to look down on the gamblers. Because of local pressure brought to bear on the Kansas legislature in 1868, Abilene's second year as a cattle town, lawmakers passed a bill, which was signed by the governor, making it illegal for anyone to set up any table or gambling device for the purpose of playing any game of chance.

Because Abilene was then on the western fringe of settlement and the town did not organize a local government with law enforcement until 1870, there was really no one to enforce the state law against gambling. This pattern was repeated in each new cattle town. Because the cattle trade was seasonal, running from spring to early fall, after the cowboys left, the gamblers and other unsavory characters left to ply their trades somewhere else until the following spring.

In Ellsworth, like most of the other cattle towns, gambling was wide open. One visitor reported in about 1872, "Gambling of every description is carried on without any attempt at privacy. I am told that there are some 75 professional gamblers in town, and every day we hear of some of their sharp tricks."

By the time the cattle trade shifted to Dodge City in 1877, the town, located in sparsely populated southwest Kansas, was ready for the trade. In fact, the year before the longhorns arrived, the town had nineteen places licensed to sell liquor. That meant that before the cowboys arrived from Texas, there was one saloon for roughly every six full-time residents of Dodge City.

The nicest and most popular saloon was the Saratoga, owned by Chalkley M. "Chalk" Beeson. He loved music and exercised good taste in providing entertainment—sometimes a full orchestra—for his customers. Other prominent saloons included the Alamo, Beaty and Kelley's Alhambra, Mueller and Straeter's Old House, the plush Opera House saloon, and the Long Branch, built in 1873 by Charles Bassett, the first sheriff in Dodge City and Ford County, and A. J. Peacock. Later Chalkley Beeson and W. H. Harris purchased the Long Branch.

In February 1883, Luke L. Short, a gambler, purchased Beeson's interest in the Long Branch saloon. Short, a native of Mississippi who grew up in North Texas, had arrived in Dodge City about a year earlier. Before that, he had trailed longhorns north from Texas, hunted buffalo for their hides, and had been a gambler in Abilene when it was a cattle town. Soon after twenty-nine-year-old Short became part owner of the Long Branch saloon, his partner, W. H. Harris, ran for mayor of Dodge City, apparently at Short's urging. At the time, Short was at odds with Nicholas B. Klaine, the editor of the *Dodge City*

The interior of the Long Branch saloon in Dodge City is very different from how it was depicted on the CBS television program *Gunsmoke*. Robert M. Wright sold the saloon to Chalkley M. Beeson in 1878. Gamblers frequented the Long Branch, but Beeson enjoyed music and at one point had an eight-piece orchestra playing nightly, to the delight of cowboys, gamblers, and others. (Courtesy Kansas State Historical Society)

Times, who was supporting another candidate, Larry Deger. Harris was defeated by Deger. The vote was 214 to 143.

Three weeks after the election, the town's new mayor and his administration passed two new ordinances. One was to suppress vice and immorality; and the other was to define and punish vagrancy. Two days after the ordinances became law, three women, prostitutes who ostensibly were employed as singers at the Long Branch saloon, were arrested. They were given the choice of taking the next east- or westbound train out of Dodge City.

Luke Short and W. C. Harris were not pleased. They did not object to the new ordinances, but they believed that the women's arrests were retaliations from the new mayor and his friends. Prostitutes in other saloons had not been arrested and treated in the same manner as the women from the Long Branch saloon.

A few hours after the three prostitutes were arrested at the Long Branch, Luke Short met L. C. Hartman, city clerk, on the street.

Hartman, a special deputy, had helped to arrest the three women and was one of the new mayor's friends. Short shot at Hartman but missed, and Hartman fired back. Fortunately, neither man was hurt. Short, however, was immediately arrested and jailed. That evening, five other gamblers were also arrested and taken to jail. They were not charged with crimes but told to take either an east- or westbound train and get out of Dodge City. They did. Luke Short and two other gamblers took an eastbound train. Short began to make plans as he rode to Kansas City. There he wrote out a petition. The next day, he traveled by train west to Topeka to present it to George W. Glick, governor of Kansas. Short explained in the document that he had been a resident of Dodge City for two years, he was a businessman, he had been forced to leave town instead of being charged with a crime, and Dodge City was a violent community in turmoil. Short then returned to Kansas City.

Governor Glick alerted two companies of the National Guard to stand by to go to Dodge City to bring law and order to the town, but they were never sent. As the governor tried to determine what was going on in Dodge City, Bat Masterson, a former sheriff there and an old friend of Short's, arrived in Kansas City. Meanwhile, Kansas newspapers had a field day reporting on the trouble at Dodge City. As public opinion began to shift against Dodge City, three prominent Dodge City businessmen traveled by train to Kansas City to talk with Short and Bat Masterson. In Topeka, the governor sent the state adjutant general to Dodge City for a firsthand look. Within a few days, things calmed down.

By early June, Luke Short and Bat Masterson headed for Dodge City. They were not alone. Several friends joined them, including Wyatt Earp, Doc Holiday, and a few other well-known gunfighters. If Short and his group hoped to intimidate the mayor, editor Klaine, and others in Dodge City, they did not succeed. Some newspapers had predicted there would be a war at Dodge City, but there was no violence.

The *Ford County Globe* told its readers that the squabble had ended peacefully: "Our city trouble is about over and things in general will be conducted as of old. All parties that were run out of town have returned and no further effort will be made to drive them away. Gambling houses, we understand, are again to be opened, but with screen

Robert M. Wright, born in Maryland in 1840, came west at the age of sixteen. In Dodge City, he became a merchant, dealer in buffalo hides, and stockman, and served as town treasurer, later as mayor, and as a representative to the Kansas legislature. He died at age eighty-nine. Unlike many other Dodge City residents, Wright was temperate in his habits, and during his last forty years in Dodge City, he went to bed before eight o'clock each night. (Courtesy Kansas State Historical Society)

doors in front of their place of business. All the warriors met Saturday night and settled their past differences and everything was made lovely and serene."

Before the year ended, Luke Short and W. C. Harris sold the Long Branch saloon and left Dodge City for Fort Worth, Texas. When Short became ill a few years later, he checked into a hotel at Geuda Springs in Sumner County, Kansas. Geuda Springs was a health resort with springs that reportedly contained health-restoring minerals. Short was suffering from dropsy. The springs did not cure him, and in less than a month, on September 8, 1893, Luke Short died. His body was shipped by train to Fort Worth, Texas, where he was buried in Oakwood Cemetery.

When Short left Dodge City late in 1883, the town returned to its old ways. Gambling flourished even though the town had ordinances against it. They were simply not enforced. The local residents wanted to make as much money as possible from the cowboys and drovers. Nearly all saloons in Dodge City offered gambling. Games of chance, however, were pretty much limited to card games such as poker, monte, and faro, and a handful of dice games, including chuck-a-luck, hazard, and keno, a game played something like bingo. Keno required many players and therefore was reserved for busy nights in the larger saloons. Fancy gambling equipment was not common, contrary to the impression sometimes conveyed by Hollywood Westerns.

Of course, the professional gamblers usually won. The Texas drovers and cowboys usually lost. Dodge City was a paradise for gamblers. Robert M. Wright, an early merchant, summarized their treatment in his book *Dodge City, the Cowboy Capital* (1913). One day a cowboy, bent on having a good time, rode into town and headed for the Green Front saloon to do some gambling. He quickly lost all his money.

Mad because he lost, the cowboy decided to prefer charges against the proprietor of the saloon for "running a gambling joint." The cowboy found Wright, then the mayor of Dodge City, introduced himself, and, according to Wright, presented his case with these words: "A feller in that 'ere Green Front has just robbed me of more'n sixteen dollars, an' I want ter have 'im pulled."

Wright replied, by his own account, "Been gambling, have you?" and called to Bill Tilghman, the city marshal, who was crossing the street. "Here, Bill, is a fellow that has been gambling. Run him in." The marshal took the cowboy to police court, where, according to Wright, he was fined ten dollars and costs, "as an object lesson to those who might presume to violate the anti-gambling ordinance of Dodge City."

Obviously the town had two standards.

When the legislature quarantined the whole state of Kansas in 1883, Dodge City ceased to be a cattle town. It marked the end of the rough-and-tumble Kansas cattle town era and the glory days of gamblers who took the Texas cowboys for as much as they could.

22

When Cowboys Went on Strike

Cowboys in the Texas Panhandle were not happy with changes made by ranchers in 1883 when they organized the Panhandle Cattlemen's Association. Several ranches had new owners who represented eastern and European investment companies. Although one purpose of the organization was to eliminate rustling, the ranchers called a halt to an old practice where cowboys could take part of their pay in calves, brand mavericks, and even run small herds on their employer's land. The ranch owners wanted to expand their holdings and increase profits.

Many cowboys did not like the changes. Several were convinced that the new ranch owners cared little about their cowboys and their welfare, and that some ranchers were taking advantage of the cowboys, their hired men on horseback.

Early in the spring of 1883, the cowboys on three large ranches—the IX, the LIT, and the LS, all in the Canadian River country of the Texas Panhandle—happened to come together near the mouth of Frio Creek east of modern Hereford, Texas. The outfits had been rounding up cattle that had drifted south during the winter. All of the men enjoyed a meal together and then began talking about their wages and the new rules being imposed on all cowhands.

Everyone voiced dissatisfaction. Because their employers had organized an association, it was only natural that the cowboys began to talk about having their own organization. Before the cowboys from the three outfits broke camp, they had formed a loose organization and issued a proclamation, the original of which can be seen today at the Panhandle-Plains Historical Museum at Canyon, Texas.

The proclamation, which was submitted to the ranch owners and announced what was the first cowboy strike in the American West, reads:

> We, the undersigned cowboys of Canadian River, do by these presents agree to bind ourselves into the following obligations, viz—First, that we will not work for less than $50 per month, and we furthermore agree no one shall work for less than $50 per month, after 31st of March.
>
> Second, good cooks shall also receive $50 per month.
>
> Third, anyone running an outfit shall not work for less than $75 per month. Anyone violating the above obligations shall suffer the consequences. Those not having funds to pay board after March 31st will be provided for 30 days at Tascosa.

The ultimatum was signed by twenty-four men, including the wagon bosses for the LX, the LIT, and the LS ranches: Roy Griffin, Waddy Peacock, and Tom Harris. The cowboys, led by Tom Harris of the LS, set April 1, 1883, as the date for their strike. They also established a small strike fund.

Exactly what happened next is a bit cloudy, but when the cowboy strike began, cowpunchers from two more ranches—the T Anchor and the LE—had joined in the walkout. Many of the striking cowboys gathered at Tascosa, where they drank and talked and drank some more. The exact number of cowboys who went on strike is not known, but it was anywhere from thirty to more than three hundred, although the number frequently changed. Some cowboys individually negotiated with the ranch owners or managers, but striking cowboys from the T-Anchor and the LE were fired. Cowboys at the LS and the LIT were offered slightly higher wages. Those that did not accept were fired. Some of the replacement workers were actually cowboys on strike who wanted to return to work. Ranch owners and managers continued with their plans for the spring roundup, and many hired replacement cowboys at temporarily higher wages.

The strike lasted more than two months, and during that time, newspapers in Colorado, Kansas, and Texas reported on it. One ac-

These LS cowboys are drinking at a bar in Tascosa, Texas. Although the photograph was taken in 1907 by Erwin E. Smith, about fourteen years after the strike, the scene was probably similar when LS cowboys and those from other ranches went on strike in 1883 and gathered in Tascosa. (Courtesy E. E. Smith Foundation)

count said the strikers planned to burn fences, attack ranches, and kill cattle, but there was no violence from either side. The strike was peaceful. Most newspaper accounts seem to have favored the ranchers, but a livestock journal in Texas took the position that some cowboys were worth "almost any money as faithful servants" and were entitled to all the money the ranchers could afford to pay. The journal, however, said it thought the ranch owners were the best and fairest judges of what they could afford.

Part IV

BUFFALO, HORSES, AND OTHER CREATURES

The fact that man knows right from wrong proves his intellectual superiority to other creatures, but the fact that he can do wrong proves his moral inferiority to any creature that cannot.
—Mark Twain

23

The Cat that Crossed the Plains

At dawn on the morning of April 2, 1850, James Philly, a tobacco grower, yoked the oxen to his wagon, then gathered his wife and three children and prepared to set out from their home at West Point in Cass County, Missouri. They were bound for California. The weather was perfect. The temperature was cool, and there were no clouds in the sky as the bright sun rose above the eastern horizon. Philly thought the weather was a good omen for the long journey of two thousand miles that lay ahead.

The family had loaded the wagon the day before. James Philly helped his wife climb into the wagon, where she made herself comfortable on the seat at the front. Their young son, George Philly, also climbed in, but his brother, Phillip, stood on the ground clinging to old Bose, his dog. Perhaps as an afterthought, the father said the dog could go along.

Then, as James Philly lifted his five-year-old daughter, May, into the wagon, she began to cry. The father asked her what was wrong. She replied, "I want Jip to go." Jip was the family's cat. The family had decided earlier to leave the cat in Missouri, but the look in the little girl's face was too much for her father. Anyway, the cat had already jumped into the wagon and was at May's feet. The parents looked at each other and smiled. They agreed to let Jip go with them to California.

The family of five with a dog and cat got under way and traveled northwest to St. Joseph, Missouri, located on the Missouri River. The town was a jumping-off point for emigrants bound west. There the Philly family joined a large wagon train and a few days later crossed the Missouri River. From there, the emigrants crossed what is today northeast Kansas and entered modern Nebraska, where they struck the Platte River and turned west along the south bank, following the already well-traveled Oregon Trail. They reached Fort Kearny on June 10.

By then, the Phillys' daily routine was pretty much like that of the other emigrants in their wagon train. They would find a suitable campsite along the trail each night, get up about dawn, have breakfast, load their cooking utensils and supplies in their wagon, and set out with the wagon train toward the west. Most days they stopped during the heat of the day—they called it nooning—had their midday meal, rested, and later in the afternoon resumed their journey, traveling until early evening, when they again camped for the night, ate their evening meal, and then went to sleep.

Their journey was uneventful as their wagon train pushed westward across the prairie and plains following the Platte River. After crossing to the North Platte, they headed in a northwestward direction toward Fort Laramie.

Back in Missouri, James Philly had been a tobacco grower. He knew well that the average tobacco user would rather go without his bread than his tobacco. So Philly took a large supply of tobacco that cost him twenty-five cents a pound, and carried it in his wagon. As men in the wagon train ran out of tobacco, Philly began selling it at one dollar per pound.

When Indians approached the emigrants wanting a handout or to trade, they learned Philly had tobacco, and he became very popular. He made some good trades. He later told a friend that the Indians wanted tobacco and whiskey more than anything else. Once or twice, when Indians surrounded the wagons in a threatening manner, Philly gave them tobacco and they left. On one occasion, after leaving Philly's train with tobacco, Indians robbed emigrants in a wagon train ahead. Philly thought the Indians viewed him as a great brave with much charm.

Philly, his wife and children, and the family dog old Bose and Jip the cat made the journey safely over the Oregon Trail to Fort Bridger, located in what is now southwest Wyoming. There they left the Oregon Trail and traveled southwest over a trail established earlier by Mormons to Salt Lake City. There James Philly sold what tobacco he had left for five dollars a pound.

From Salt Lake City, the emigrants headed west across the desert to the Humboldt River. Before they reached the stream's headwaters, many of the emigrants' oxen died from the heat and a lack of water. Other oxen became weak and gave out. They were left along the trail. Even the emigrants ran low on rations, and people in the wagon train were almost reduced to starvation.

By the time the wagon train reached the Humboldt River, Jame Philly's daughter, May, who had become the pet of nearly everyone else in the train, was nothing but skin and bones. She became so weak and frail that she could not eat the coarse food, which was all the emigrants had left.

One morning, Philly and his wife found a rabbit at the door of their tent. They dressed and cooked it for May. Where the rabbit came from was a mystery, but the next morning, there was another rabbit at the tent door. For the next two weeks, while the emigrants traveled south along the Humboldt River, almost every morning, there was a dead rabbit at the entrance to Philly's tent.

James Philly found out where the rabbits came from. One morning at dawn, he watched through the tent flap and saw Jip, their faithful house cat, bringing the carcass to the tent. The cat apparently had found the rabbits in the grass and other vegetation growing under the willow trees that lined the banks of the Humboldt River.

When the emigrants left the Humboldt for the Carson River, they had to cross the forty-mile desert, a dreaded portion of the trail that ended at what was known as Ragtown. It really was not a town but a stopping point where there was plenty of water and shade. Someone at Ragtown offered James Philly one hundred dollars for Jip the cat. Philly refused to sell the cat, believing it had saved his daughter's life.

Near the end of their journey, young George Philly became ill and died. His little body was wrapped in a blanket and laid in a narrow grave beneath a large pine tree. The boy's father marked the grave with two large stakes of wood and then piled on it many large rocks and stones. The mother, already frail from the hardships of the long journey, was in deep sorrow and could hardly stand. After a brief ceremony conducted by others in the wagon train, everyone continued their journey a short distance and camped for the night with Jip, the cat, and old Bose, the dog.

Next morning, James Philly could not find old Bose. On a hunch, Philly returned to George's grave and found the faithful dog guarding it. During the night, the dog had returned to the grave, only to be met by a band of wolves apparently intent upon digging up the grave. Old Bose was badly injured by the wolves when he tried to drive them away. James Philly carefully carried the injured dog back to camp, where he was tenderly cared for. The dog died many years later at Dutch Flat in Placer County, California, where the family first settled.

As for Jip the cat, he also lived a long life and apparently died a natural death. James Philly died in Santa Barbara, where he and his wife later moved. His wife died in Santa Rosa, at the home of little May, who had since married. As for Phillip Philly, he lived to be an old man and died early in the twentieth century.

24

Marsh Johnson's First
Buffalo Hunt

It was March 1867 when young Marsh Johnson told his father and mother that he was leaving their farm home near Fort Worth, Texas, to get rich in the cattle business. A few days earlier, nineteen-year-old Johnson had met John Hittson, a well-known rancher from Callahan County, located in the rolling plains region east of modern Abilene, Texas. Hittson, better known as "Captain Jack," and his right-hand man, John Clarke, had come to Fort Worth to buy thirty-five horses to replace those stolen less than a month earlier by Comanche Indians. Hittson, apparently impressed with young Johnson, offered him a job on the condition that he would receive only his board until he learned cowboying. Johnson accepted the terms.

It took several days for Hittson and Clarke to locate the kind of horses they wanted. Good horses were scarce. "The Civil War and the thieving Indians had caused a shortage. At the time a good pony could be bought for twenty-five dollars and a good horse for around forty," recalled Johnson.

After the horses were purchased, Johnson said good-bye to his parents and left. Hittson, Clarke, and Johnson rode out of Fort Worth, herding the horses and leading a packhorse loaded with supplies toward Callahan County, located about one hundred sixty-five miles to the west.

John Hittson, thirty-six, was a native of Tennessee who moved to Texas with his parents in 1847. Four years later, Hittson married and moved; he helped organize Palo Pinto County, where he was elected sheriff. He held the office until the Civil War began. It was then that Hittson moved west and settled at Camp Cooper, an abandoned U.S. Army post located on the Clear Fork of the Brazos River in what is now south central Throckmorton County. There during the Civil War John Hittson branded mavericks—cattle without brands—and sold them in Mexico.

Despite several narrow escapes from hostile Indians, Hittson maintained his ranching headquarters at the fort during most of the Civil War. When peace came in 1865, Hittson was the wealthiest man in the region. The following year, Hittson moved his ranch headquarters farther west to Callahan County and let his cattle graze the open range of eight counties. By then, his operation was called the Three Circles Ranch.

In March 1867, Hittson, Clarke, and young Marsh Johnson were driving the horses to Callahan County. It was the first time Johnson had traveled west of Fort Worth. He later recalled, "After living in the timber for several years, the wide rolling prairie was a revelation to me and on the last day of the journey, there was nothing to obstruct the view. Desolate? Yes, to one who could not see beauty in rolling sand, sagebrush, and mesquite brushes, but the spell of enchantment held me slave that day for I was seeking adventure from out of these wide-open spaces. The quietness of the range was striking to view in every direction the same. The open prairie with its immeasurable horizon seemed to roll on and on as endless as the sea."

Late one afternoon, as the men herded the horses westward, they spotted fast-moving objects in the distance, scurrying about the sagebrush. As they moved closer, they could see two javelinas, or Mexican wild hogs, battling. In color, javelinas are kind of a spotted gray with long, razor-sharp tusks. If pursued or cornered, they are extremely dangerous. Moving closer, the men stopped and watched, amazed at the fury they were seeing.

"On and on they fought, first one and then the other the victor," recalled Johnson. "Like a flash they rolled over and over toward us until they were within two feet of one of our horses. At once their death grip released, and they separated. The next instant the larger hog flew in a frenzy and attacked the horse with his tusks and almost severed a front leg. Without warning a well-aimed bullet ended the career of that hog. We were compelled to kill the horse as he was so badly wounded he could not travel and possibly would never be any good for service."

It took several days for the men herding the horses to reach Hittson's ranch headquarters. They camped out at night, taking turns watching and guarding the horses and outfit. Johnson learned that each stop was carefully planned in order to reach water by the time they needed it for man and beast. He also learned to spread down on the ground one blanket for a bed and one for a cover. Johnson learned to awake easily and at an instant's notice.

Two ranch hands welcomed Hittson, Clarke, and Johnson. Greetings were short, and Hittson introduced Johnson to the others by name with no explanation. They unsaddled their horses and silently carried the provisions they had brought on the packhorse into the shack. They found a few beans in a huge iron pot suspended over a campfire and a chunk of barbecue for their supper. After they ate, the men talked for a while as they sat around the campfire. When Johnson learned wild buffalo were about as plentiful as cattle on the nearby open range, he said he had never hunted buffalo. John Clarke said he would take him hunting the next day.

The next morning, at the first light of dawn in a cloudless sky, Johnson and Clarke got up. "We could hardly wait until the coffee was made and the 'pone' of bread in the Dutch oven was pronounced done," remembered Johnson, who said they needed no second call from Andy, the cook, to "come git it." After hurriedly gulping down black coffee, a piece of bread, and some meat, Johnson and Clarke mounted their horses and rode off to the northwest in search of buffalo. Clarke cautioned Johnson to be constantly on the alert for Indians.

The two men had traveled about two miles from the ranch headquarters when they sighted two buffalo cows and an old bull grazing on the slope of a hill. Johnson recalled, "This was my first sight of a buffalo, and so excited was I . . . that my heart seemed to crawl up in my throat—a real, live, wild buffalo! Kill them buffalo? Certainly we intended to bag every one of them." Johnson and Clarke, mounted on their horses, watched the buffalo and talked about what to do next.

They decided a bold charge was better and more honorable than sneaking up and shooting the animals. The buffalo were nearly half a mile away. "We decided to make the charge from where we stood. We wanted to do the thing right or not at all, so we charged. Think of two gosling green boys and two poor shabby Texas ponies with practically no gun worth 'toting,' making a charge on a herd of buffalo at that distance and you will realize what chance we had in killing one that day," wrote Johnson.

Johnson had an old Colt six-shooter that had been used during the Civil War, while Clarke had an old pepperbox six-shooter, the barrel of which was simply a round piece of steel, or pot metal, about the size and shape of an oyster can, only longer, with six holes drilled in it lengthwise, similar to a honeycomb. It, too, shot the cap and ball, and took nearly a half-hour to reload. It did not fire two shots at once, and sometimes it did not fire at all.

Apparently by accident, the two young men charged upwind toward the buffalo. The animals did not sense the charge until Johnson and Clarke were within seventy-five yards. By then, however, their ponies were about exhausted. The buffalo, in poor shape, started to run. What happened next is told in Johnson's own words:

> We were now on the firing line so to speak and pop, pop went the old rusty pistols, when we could get them to go off, but somehow we didn't kill them as fast as we intended. It was a running fight and I suggested to Clarke that we concentrate our fire on the old bull who had by this time stopped running and defied us with a shake of his horns, followed by a savage charge at us which changed the complexion of what we were looking for. Our ponies were run down, our ammunition about gone, and that old bull had been worked up to a frenzy—our chances of escape began to look slim.
>
> By this time I had decided that a buffalo has temper. This one certainly had no idea of retreating, but I was beginning to look for a safe place. The bull made several charges at us and we could only dodge from one mesquite bush to another. With a scrape of his hoof in the dry dust, and a snort of his extended nostrils, he approached first one of us, then the other. I had fired and fired in vain at the animal and had only one load in my pistol left. Clarke's ammunition was exhausted. I intended to execute a death sentence on the bull with this bullet. I knew that if I could get him to charge me while up in one of those small mesquite trees, I

could shoot him in the loins and kill him. Finally the bull made the charge I was wanting, and as I climbed up the tree he barely missed catching me on his horns. I fired my last shot into his loins, over the kidneys, and he bit the dust—the fight was over. I climbed down from the mesquite tree and examined my trophy. He was too poor to be eaten by the coyotes and his hide was not fit to grace a chair bottom so we slowly mounted our horses and rode home.

Marsh Johnson became a cowboy, and during the years that followed, he killed hundreds of buffalo. Years later, when he was about eighty-six years old, he wrote that no other buffalo excited him as much as that first old bull he killed in 1867 on the rolling plains of west Texas.

25

The White Stallion of the Plains

It was the evening of June 20, 1843. About ninety U.S. dragoons, under the command of Captain Nathan Boone, the youngest son of Daniel Boone, were camped on the south bank of the Arkansas River near the mouth of Walnut Creek in what is now Barton County, Kansas. After finishing their evening meal, they watched a beautiful sunset and then gathered around their campfires to talk. As the last light of day disappeared on the broad western horizon, they heard in the distance the neighing and snorting of horses and the barking and howling of wolves. No one in camp knew what the sounds meant except Captain Boone, who said there must be a battle of wild horses and wolves. The dragoons' horses became restless, and a few tried to break loose and run. To prevent a stampede, Captain Boone ordered the guard doubled around the horses, and everyone but the guards went to sleep.

Twenty-four days earlier, Captain Boone and his dragoons had ridden out of Fort Gibson in Indian Territory, now eastern Oklahoma. Boone and his mounted soldiers were under orders "to make a reconnaissance" of the plains in what is present-day Oklahoma and southern Kansas as far north as the great bend of the Arkansas River. All four lieutenants in Boone's command were West Point graduates. One of them was Abraham Buford, a twenty-three-year-old Kentuckian, who less than two years before had graduated from West Point.

At daylight the next morning, Captain Boone told Buford and two other lieutenants to take some men and capture a wild horse or two. The lieutenants were Buford, Richard H. Anderson, a native of South Carolina, and Robert H. Chilton, a native of Virginia. The three officers selected three squads of the best mounted dragoons and moved down Walnut Creek toward the sound of the neighing and barking, which had continued during the night and early morning.

As they traveled about a mile under cover of the banks along Walnut Creek, the noise grew louder. It was coming from the level plains ahead. About three hundred yards from the bluffs of Walnut Creek, the dragoons halted. Buford, Anderson, and Chilton dismounted and climbed the creek bank to reconnoiter.

"We saw the battle raging; the herd of horses was about 150 strong and the most prominent one among them was the 'Great White horse of the plains.' He seemed to be the commander, and had formed the mares in a circle with their heels to the enemy, or outward. The diameter of this was about 100 yards, with all the foals and younger colts in the center; all the stallions, with the 'white horse' in command, on the outside and surrounding the circle of mares, which were fighting the wolves," recalled Buford, a big man who stood more than six feet tall.

Now the "Great White horse of the plains" mentioned by Buford was already something of a legend on the western plains from Texas northward. There was undoubtedly more than one wild white stallion on the plains, but tales of the animal eluding capture had already become part of western lore when Buford saw the animal. Perhaps the earliest account of a wild white stallion appears in Washington Irving's *A Tour of the Prairies* (1835), in which he relates stories he heard from frontiersmen in 1831 about such a wild horse in what is today northern Oklahoma and southern Kansas that could pace "faster than the fleetest horse can run." That was twelve years before Buford and the other officers came on the white stallion in 1843.

Josiah Gregg, in his classic *Commerce of the Prairies*, written during the early 1840s, observed that he had heard "marvelous tales" of a "medium-sized mustang stallion of perfect symmetry, milk-white, save a pair of black ears, a natural pacer." Gregg wrote that "the trapper celebrates him in the northern Rocky Mountains; the hunter on the Arkansas; while others have him pacing on the borders of Texas."

After watching the stallion and other horses battling the wolves, Buford and the other officers decided to chase the wolves away and capture some of the horses. They crawled down the bank, mounted their horses, and signaled their squads to follow. They charged onto the plains as fast as their horses could go.

The wolves quickly retreated. As for the horses, the white stallion commanded the rear guard. "Before the horses retreated, I noticed a squad of stallions approach the circle of mares; they pawed the earth, neighed and snorted fiercely and started off, leading the retreat. The mares opened the circle, and the colts went out following a squad of mares, and other mares in their rear, and the 'white horse' still in the rear," remembered Buford, who was mounted on a Kentucky thoroughbred horse given to him by his father, a noted Kentucky breeder of thoroughbreds and shorthorn cattle. The horse had been sired by Sidi Hamet, a legendary stallion in Kentucky horse circles. Buford recalled that he gave his horse, named Cid, the spur and raced toward the white stallion "with pistol in hand." Buford wanted to crease the horse's neck if he could get close enough.

"During this chase Anderson's squad and mine kept well together," recalled Buford. "But Chilton's men being mounted on inferior horses, such as Noah's ponies, were left far in the rear. As we approached the herd the 'white horse' would go slow and let us come up to within 20 yards of him, but could go away from us at his ease. He would keep between us and some of the old mares and colts until we would drive him forward by approaching too close."

As Buford related many years later, "When it became evident that some of these mares and colts would fall into our hands, the 'white horse,' evidently with much excitement, would abandon them to their fate. We continued this chase some six or seven miles, when all of our horses, save my horse Cid, were pretty well blown. I made several forced dashes at the 'white horse,' but could not reach him. Cid was too heavily handicapped, although my avoirdupois was not near so great as it is today, when the 'white horse' was only carrying a feather."

That June day in 1843, Buford, Anderson, and Chilton and their men captured several old mares and colts. Unfortunately, as Buford recalled, Lieutenant Anderson "attempted to crease a young stallion that he got along side of, but sent the ball through his brain and killed him. Creasing is sending a ball through the upper muscle of the neck, which stuns the horse and he falls and is helpless for a few minutes, and can be secured by a lariat while in this condition."

As Buford and the others started back toward their camp with the wild horses they had captured, they crossed the area where the horses and wolves had done battle. There they saw quite a number of dead wolves and horses and some carcasses of horses on the outer edge of the battlefield, where they had fallen in some of the charges. The wolves had devoured their carcasses.

When Buford and the others returned to camp, they found Captain Boone and the other dragoons roasting buffalo hump and making jerky. Buford remembered that when they arrived in camp with the old mares and colts, Boone laughed heartily, and said, "Why, Medoc (which was my nickname among the officers,) I thought you were going to capture the 'white horse.' mounted on your thorough-bred from the Bluegrass region?" Buford continued, "My reply was that Cid was too heavily handicapped, while the 'white horse' was without weight."

Buford, Anderson, Chilton, and their men were tired after the chase. They ordered the release of the wild horses the dragoons had captured so they could rejoin the herd. The officers then enjoyed the buffalo hump, roasted before the open fire, and got a good night's sleep under the stars. The next morning, Captain Boone and his men resumed their journey back to Fort Gibson, where they arrived on the last day of July 1843.

Buford never saw the white stallion again, but he recounted his experience many times during the rest of his life. Buford was promoted to first lieutenant in 1846 and was brevetted captain for gallantry at Buena Vista. From 1848 to 1851, he served in New Mexico; between 1852 and 1854 in the cavalry school at Carlisle, Pennsylvania; and as secretary of the military asylum of Harrodsburg, Kentucky, with the rank of captain. On October 22, 1854, he resigned from the army and purchased Bosque Bonita, a bluegrass farm, in Woodford County, Kentucky. He soon became known for the horses and cattle produced there until early in the Civil War. Although Buford loved the Union, he was a staunch believer in states' rights and became so irritated with federal constraints and regulations that he joined the Confederate army, in which he was commissioned a brigadier general in 1862. He saw much action until the war ended, when he returned to his Kentucky bluegrass farm, where he resumed breeding thoroughbreds. By then, Buford weighed three hundred pounds. Bosque Bonita became well known among horsemen for Buford's lavish hospitality. The deaths of his son in 1872 and his wife in 1879 caused him much sadness. After financial reverses cost him his farm and horses, he shot himself in 1884 while visiting a nephew in Danville, Indiana.

26

Wild Buffalo and Other Critters

Life on the plains and prairies of the West has changed. The truly wild horses are gone, as are the wild elk, wolves, and most of the bears except those preserved by states or the federal government. No longer does one see wild buffalo in vast numbers, but many exist in private and government herds. It is rare, except perhaps in New Mexico and a few other scattered areas, to run across mountain lions, although in recent years, there have been isolated reports of cougars (also called panthers, pumas, and catamounts) in some areas where the hand of man is not in great evidence.

The glory days of a variety of large wild animals disappeared when the white man settled the plains and prairies. Today many smaller varieties of wild animals can still be seen in many areas along rivers and creeks and in pockets of trees. Coyotes, possum, raccoons, wildcats, jackrabbits, prairie dogs, skunks, gofers, badgers, armadillos, beaver, wood rats, and mice are numerous, along with many songbirds, hawks, and owls in favorable habitat. However, the glory days of America's nineteenth-century wildlife are long gone.

Probably the most interesting animal for the early white men crossing the plains and prairie was the bison, commonly called buffalo. William Becknell, the man who opened trade with Santa Fe in 1821, tells us little about the buffalo except that on his second journey in 1822, crossing the Cimarron Desert, he and his men had to kill a buffalo for the water in the animal's stomachs.

Two years later, as Meredith M. Marmaduke and a party of Missourians were heading for Santa Fe, they came upon countless buffalo. On June 10, 1824, Marmaduke wrote in his journal: "Saw this day at least ten thousand buffalo, the prairies were literally covered with them for many miles. Killed 9 buffalo today."

George Sibley, another early traveler, reported similar scenes between 1825 and 1827 while he was surveying and marking the Santa Fe Trail. On one occasion, Sibley wrote that during the night his party's horses "took fright." He added, "The cause could not be ascertained, tho' it was probably a Wolf or a Buffalo." Sibley noted that at that time in the area he crossed buffalo were scarce, but for the most part, the hunters with Sibley's expedition had no difficulty finding enough buffalo to kill for food.

In areas where wood was scarce, the travelers often used buffalo dung for fuel. A few old-timers claimed that one did not need to use pepper on food cooked over a hot fire fueled with buffalo chips.

When Thomas Farnham followed the Santa Fe Trail in 1839, he and his party spent three days moving through what apparently was one very large herd of buffalo. Farnham wrote:

> It appeared oftentimes extremely dangerous even for the immense cavalcade of the Santa Fe traders to attempt to break its way through them. We traveled at the rate of 15 miles a day. Fifteen times three equals forty-five. Take forty-five times thirty and you get 1350 square miles of country so thickly covered with the noble animals, that when viewed from a height it scarcely afforded a sight of a square league of its surface.

There are many other accounts describing vast herds of buffalo on the plains and prairie, leaving no doubt that thousands, perhaps millions, of the shaggy animals once roamed the West. Contemporary accounts indicate that they were fascinating wild animals to watch.

Some travelers thought they were ugly when first seeing them. A buffalo's head, especially a bull's large head and forequarters, make him appear out of proportion to his hindquarters. This may be why first impressions of the animal can be negative. Most early travelers, however, seem to have changed their minds after taking time to watch the buffalo. The animal is a magnificent-looking creature in spite of its odd build.

Observers learned that buffalo usually went to water once or twice a day. When water was scarce, they could and often did go without water for several days—much longer than domestic cattle. Although there are countless stories about thirsty buffalo, one of the best was told by George Ruxton, an Englishman who crossed the plains and prairie in the 1840s. Ruxton was about to make camp one evening when three buffalo bulls came up from a nearby river where they had been drinking. They leisurely walked in front of Ruxton, moving slowly and stopping frequently. They paid no attention to the Englishman.

Ruxton recalled that one of the buffalo kept lying down on the ground whenever the other two animals stopped. Curious, he followed the three buffalo. When two of the buffalo stopped again and looked back at Ruxton, the third animal lay down again. He lay on the prairie grass as Ruxton rode up on horseback within a few feet of the animal. Only then did it get up and slowly follow the other buffalo. Ruxton decided to see just how close he could get to the drowsy buffalo.

Taking his rifle, Ruxton dismounted and slowly moved toward the animal, who by then had stopped again. The bull never looked around as Ruxton walked up and placed his hand on its rump. The bull paid no attention to Ruxton and again lay down on the grass. Ruxton killed the buffalo. When he butchered the carcass for his evening meal, he was surprised to find the animal's stomach completely full of water; apparently this made the animal sleepy.

Next to accounts of buffalo, early travelers made reference to deer and "goats." The latter were pronghorns that were later determined to be the fastest land mammal in North America. Pronghorns, found nowhere else in the world, are the only mammals with branched horns that shed them. Pronghorns, sometimes called "prairie ghosts," usually ran as humans approached. They are capable of sustained speeds of thirty-five to sixty miles per hour. Scientists later determined that pronghorns are capable of seeing movement several miles away.

Early travelers, however, provided little detail on pronghorns and on the next most common wild animals—wolves and prairie dogs—seen on the prairies and plains.

Josiah Gregg devotes a chapter to animals and other creatures in the second volume of his classic *Commerce of the Prairies* (1844). Gregg was fascinated by the countless prairie dogs he saw living in what some travelers described as "dog towns." Gregg told of seeing some prairie dog towns that covered several square miles. "They generally locate upon fine dry plains, coated with fine short grass, upon which they feed," he wrote, adding that small owls and rattlesnake also lived in the prairie dog burrows.

Aside from passing reference to these animals, rattlesnakes seem to be second to the buffalo in mention. Gregg saw numerous rattlesnakes and wrote that "they are exceedingly abundant upon these plains: Scores of them are sometimes killed in the course of a day's travel; yet they seem remarkably harmless, for I have never witnessed an instance of a man being bitten, though they have been known to crawl, even into the beds of travelers. Mules are sometimes bitten by them, yet very rarely, though they must daily walk over considerable numbers."

George Sibley, like Gregg, makes several references to rattlesnakes in his journal. Near the Arkansas River in modern-day Kansas, Sibley wrote, "Our road this evening lay over some tolerably rough sandy ground, in which rattle snakes are very numerous." The following day, Sibley wrote: "One of the mules bit by a rattle snake this evening. These snakes are very numerous & troublesome here."

Another plainsman, James R. Mead, hunting along the Smoky Hill River in modern-day Kansas in the late 1850s, told of coming upon more than twenty buffalo near the riverbank. "Standing a little distance away I noticed a buffalo calf seemingly in a very stupid condition. On walking up to him I found his head was swollen to about twice its natural size. His eyes were swollen shut so that he could not see, and to get him out of his misery I killed him with my knife. Shortly afterwards in going down the bank of the river to get a drink, I saw a yellow diamond rattlesnake about four feet long and about as large as my arm, which I also killed. This explained to me what was the matter with the calf."

For some time Mead survived on the plains by cooking most of the animals he killed. He wrote that he found "coon [raccoon] and badger very good if properly dressed and prepared. Beaver tasted too much like the bark on which they subsist, while prairie dogs are most excellent when fat and young, and their oil is very good for guns and gun locks, never gumming and only congealing in freezing weather." There was a small reptile that also caused travelers some concern until they found it to be harmless. It was the horned frog or horned lizard. Josiah Gregg called it "the most famed and curious reptile of the plains." Found in dry regions, the little creature lived on ants and other insects, but Gregg claimed they could live on air. He wrote that he once took a pair of horned frogs in a box to an eastern city, where they lived for several months before they died. During the time Gregg kept them in the box, they refused the food or water that he often offered them.

Interestingly, of all the wildlife mentioned in early narratives of travelers on the plains and prairie, birds and fowl seem to receive the least attention, although they were seen in most areas. As a general rule, the more educated the observer, the more attention paid to birds and fowl, but bird-watching was not then the art it is today, and many references to birds leave some doubt as to what the travelers were seeing or hearing. Wild turkeys, however, were clearly identified and could be found in areas with trees and along brushy creeks on the prairie. Prairie chickens, as grouse were called, were also found in many areas, as were geese and ducks. Gregg found them near the streams. He added that flocks of ravens often followed travelers.

Many of the larger wild creatures of the nineteenth century are gone, but those that remain are reminders of the glory days on the plains and prairie.

27

Tales of Legless Critters

My father told me one evening; when he was a Boy He could
Crack a Harmless Garter Snakes head off, by taking it
By the Tail, and crack it like a whip.
And so one Day I was crossing the Prairie and came on to a
Harmless Milk Snake about three feet long
I had nothing to kill it with; and thought I would
Try Cracking his head off.
The snake was going into a hole, and I grabbed its tail,
Pulled him out of his hole, and swung him around like
an Ox Whip, and when I reversed and undertook
to crack his Head Off—
I only Succeeded in wrapping it around my neck
I was very much Frightened; and so was the Snake
I Quickly Jerked it off, and killed it with my feet.
That was the First and Last, time I ever tried to crack
a snakes Head off by the Tail.

These words in this form were written by Harry Jasper Harris about
1900. Harris, a native of Connecticut, came west during the late
1850s, when snakes were so plentiful in some areas that settlers considered them pests, much like mice today. Harris's simple tale is typical of many such snake stories recalled by early settlers on the western
plains and prairies.

Although Indians had roamed the Great Plains long before the
white man arrived, most Indians did not kill snakes. The superstitious

Osages and Kansa did not even kill rattlesnakes. They believed it might make the snake tribe of Indians further north mad. Other tribes had similar beliefs. Thus when the white man arrived and began settling parts of the plains and prairie lands, snakes were plentiful. They were everywhere, and many were killed.

For the pioneer woman, the sight of a snake in her parlor was usually accepted as another of the inconveniences and drawbacks of frontier life. When she saw a snake, she usually killed it. One pioneer mother told how she killed her first rattler:

> Returning from the woods one day with an armful of sticks, I saw a large snake lying across the path in front of my three year old daughter who was with me. I caught and pushed her behind me, then throwing down my sticks, picking out the largest as I did, I went for the snake. The stick was rotten and broke with my first stroke. It enraged the rattler. He coiled himself up on one side of the path, and, rearing his head two or three feet from the ground, ran out a red forked tongue and made such a noise with his rattles that my other daughter in our cabin nearby ran to the door to see what it was.
>
> Without taking my eyes off the snake I called to her to get the hoe. She ran around and came up behind us with it. Then, without moving my tracks I took the hoe and made short work with his snakeship. We dragged him up to the house and cut off the rattles, sixteen in number, and measured him. He was over five feet in length and as large around as a man's arm.

Another time a settler's wife was cleaning their cabin when she saw a large snake on a log just behind the family clock on a rude shelf. The woman did not dare strike the snake. She would have hit the clock and probably damaged it. "Clocks were too scarce to be broken for a snake," she later recalled. So she grabbed the snake by the tail, and with a quick and strong jerk, she dashed its head on the carpetless floor. It did not hurt the sod floor, but it killed the snake.

During the 1850s, a settler built a cabin on the edge of a wooded area near Three Mile Creek close to where Junction City, Kansas, stands today. The inside of the cabin was lined with unbleached muslin. Unfortunately, it made a good hiding place for snakes. When the settler would spot a snake moving behind the muslin, he would stab it with his pitchfork, loose the muslin at the bottom, and remove the dead snake. He did not keep track of how many he killed, but his wife later recalled, "Blacksnakes, rattlers and many other kinds thus met their death."

When it came time for the annual fall housecleaning, many a settler's wife would find snakes in the most unexpected places. Sometimes they might be found in the rafters or behind furniture or under a bed. One woman, in the 1860s, found a large rattlesnake wrapped around the leather straps inside the family pump organ. "That's why the thing had seemed so hard to pump," she said after killing the four-foot snake.

Homesteaders plowing up the land often found snake eggs in the turned earth. "They were oval in shape," reported one Nebraska homesteader, adding, "and they were about the size of large beans, and I think they were attached together. The little snakes in them were about an inch or so long. The hatched snakes would run into their mother's mouth when discovered."

There's one tale about an old plainsman called Jack Stillwell—his real name was Charles—who one day found himself and a friend hiding from Indians in a buffalo wallow. A large rattlesnake crawled into the wallow and headed straight for the two men. Both men froze. If they tried to kill the snake, the noise might be heard by the nearby Indians. If they did not act, the snake might bite one or both men. An idea suddenly came to Stillwell. He was chewing tobacco. As the snake moved closer, Stillwell expectorated a mouthful of tobacco juice all over the snake's eyes and head. The unwelcome visitor turned and crawled dejectedly out of the wallow. Not long afterward, the Indians left the area, and the two men, who had remained undetected, went on their way.

People were bitten by snakes. If the snake was poisonous, they might die, but then there were the lucky ones. One warm spring day, a young girl ran to her mother, crying. She said a snake had bitten her on the foot. The mother examined the child's foot. It was not injured. But when the mother looked at the little girl's shoe, she found the marks of a snake's fangs on the heel. The stiff leather had been too hard to pierce.

When a man was bitten by a rattler, death was a possibility but not a certainty. Some men looked forward to the "cure." "Red eye" was recommended for snakebite. Aside from whiskey, some men resorted to a cure of placing gunpowder in the wound and then burning it. This cure is credited to Kit Carson, the early plainsman.

Kit Carson is credited with the snakebite cure of placing a small amount of gunpowder in the wound and then burning it. Born Christopher Houston Carson in 1809 near Boonesborough, Kentucky, he came west in about 1826. He became a mountain man, hunter, guide, Indian agent, military officer, and trader before his death at Fort Lyon, Colorado, in 1868. (Courtesy Western History Collections, University of Oklahoma Libraries)

"I cut the bite open and put flash powder in it three times and it is all right," Carson is quoted as saying. "One of my men was once bitten on the hand by a big rattler. I cut it open, flashed powder in it three times, and that afternoon he killed and scalped two Injuns."

One of the most unusual snake tales concerns a train that old-timers claimed was stalled by rattlesnakes. It seems that in a cut through much rock a few miles east of Santa Rosa on the plains in east-central New Mexico, a train had to stop when it hit a bunch of rattlesnakes on the tracks. The wheels of the engine killed many of the rattlers and the train's crew killed, by actual count, fifty-six of the snakes. The rails, holding the sun's warmth, had attracted the snakes late in the day when the train came through.

Perhaps the most unbelievable snake tale set somewhere in eastern Wyoming or western Nebraska was told by Harry Gant:

> While riding in from the west one evening at a point where I was about to drop off the rimrock to the west, I heard a loud buzzing sound and followed my ears to a pocket under some bit rocks. There I saw the rendezvous of what appeared to be at least a thousand rattlesnakes, all twisted and snarled together. They

S.Wilburn,
Scout
Master,
and 17 boy
scouts,
killed 28
rattle-snakes
in one day
near Del Rio,
Texas, 1921.
Length, from
three to six
feet, each

Rattlesnake hunting was a popular sport in the Old West. This photograph shows twenty-eight rattlers strung up like fish after they were killed by seventeen Boy Scouts and scoutmaster S. Wilburn near Del Rio, Texas, in 1921. The snakes range in length from three to six feet. (Courtesy Western History Collections, University of Oklahoma Libraries)

were having an orgy such as cannot be described, not knowing who was whose partner, nor caring. I was always getting off my horse to kill a rattler, so here was a chance to really kill some snakes. I emptied all my cartridges into the mass and then threw some big rocks into it. That didn't even make one snake leave the party.

When I later told Decker [a friend] about the sight, he said: "Where have you been? Somewhere where they had a lot of whiskey? Those booze hounds are the only ones who see snakes like that." I insisted that he go with me to the spot next morning. We took a couple of shovels and found a dozen or so dead rattle-snakes and some cripples. The party had eventually moved to another spot or else they had called it a day. Within a half mile circle, we chopped off the heads of probably a hundred cripples trying to get back to their homes in the rock crannies and prairie dog holes. We couldn't find the main outfit and Decker wouldn't believe me as to the number involved. But if I had had a couple of sticks of dynamite when I first saw them, I could have been St. Patrick II.

28

The Missing White Buffalo

In the summer of 1870, James Morgan and his brother John were hunting buffalo on the plains of far northwest Kansas near the Colorado border. It was a clear day with a bright blue sky. There was a gentle breeze blowing up from the south. It was warm but not hot. Buffalo were plentiful, and killing them for their hides had become something of a routine for the two men. That day, however, the routine was broken.

The two men were sneaking up on a large herd of shaggies when suddenly they stopped. There, ahead of them, was a white buffalo, an albino, grazing on the edge of the herd. Forgetting the rest of the buffalo, the two men quickly returned to their horses, mounted, and started for the white buffalo.

The herd ran and the two men chased the white buffalo. Within minutes, James Morgan shot and killed the animal. As they examined the white buffalo, it was John Morgan who told his brother the hide must be valuable. The next morning, they loaded the skin and the animal's head in their wagon and headed for Denver, where the buffalo was mounted by a taxidermist.

For several years, the mounted white buffalo was exhibited in various towns and cities. In 1875, the Morgan brothers got tired of traveling and showing the animal, so they placed their white buffalo in storage in Kansas City, Missouri. There it remained for several months. In Topeka, however, some officials decided the mounted white buffalo would be a great attraction at the 1876 Centennial Exhibition in Philadelphia.

Kansas officials got in touch with John Morgan, who then lived in Strong City, Kansas, and he gave them permission to ship the buffalo east. In Philadelphia, it attracted much attention. Newspapers carried stories about it, and many of them found their way back to Kansas. In Topeka and across the state, Kansans, as they sometimes do, decided that if folks in the East thought the white buffalo was something special, it must really be. Thus, when the mounted buffalo was returned to Kansas, Morgan agreed to let officials display it at the statehouse in Topeka. There it was placed in a glass case near Old Barney, another stuffed but normally colored buffalo, in the Kansas State Agricultural office.

One Kansas lawmaker, Hill P. Wilson, impressed by the trophy and the publicity it had received in the East, decided that the state should buy it. Wilson introduced a bill to buy the trophy in the Kansas legislature. But when the measure finally reached the Ways and Means Committee, members decided to offer only fifty dollars for the mounted animal.

When John Morgan heard this, he laughed. "No," he snorted, "I wouldn't even consider thinking about selling the buffalo for that. Why, P. T. Barnum says he wants it for his museum. He's already offered $1,500 for the specimen."

Whether Barnum actually had made an offer or whether John Morgan was only trying to get the politicians to increase their offer is not known. What happened next is not too clear either. History does not record that Morgan sold the buffalo to Barnum or to anyone else. As a matter of fact, James Morgan's white buffalo remained in the Kansas State Agricultural office at Topeka for several years afterward. During that time John Morgan died. His brother James had died earlier.

By 1898, the mounted white buffalo had become just another object gathering dust and taking up space in the state office. Few people paid any attention to it. No one objected one day when someone confiscated the glass case that had protected the trophy. The white buffalo was then placed in the open on top of the glass case that contained Old Barney, the other stuffed buffalo.

Sometime later, a Topeka newspaper reporter happened by the office and saw the animal in its decaying condition. He wrote an article condemning the negligence of authorities in allowing the relic to be destroyed. The reporter wrote that "mice and moth lunch off the hide continually."

A few days later, apparently as a result of the newspaper story, a woman walked into the office and claimed the mounted white buffalo. She said her husband had killed the animal years earlier. Officials, taking the woman at her word, were glad to let her cart off the old mounted animal, mice, moths, and all.

Officials forgot about the trophy until early in 1903, when a daughter of James Morgan visited Topeka and asked to see the white buffalo that her father had killed. Officials tried to explain. When Morgan's daughter asked for the name of the woman who had taken the trophy, no one had it. The daughter threatened an investigation, but the white buffalo was gone. So far as is known, James Morgan's white buffalo has never been located.

29

Grizzly and Black Bear Tales

Indian legends plus accounts left by early explorers, mountain men, and traders leave no doubt that black bears and even grizzly bears once roamed the western plains and prairies in significant numbers. The black bears, smaller than the grizzly and lacking the hump just behind the shoulder, roamed much of the eastern portion of the plains and prairie lands; some may still be found there today in isolated areas. The grizzly, however, preferred the high plains region east of the Rockies. It can be said that during the days when countless buffalo roamed the plains and prairies, grizzly bears could usually be found following the herds.

Probably the first recorded account of a grizzly was made by Meriwether Lewis and William Clark on the plains of what is now North Dakota. The explorers had heard about the animal from Indians, who told of its strength and ferocity. Naturally, members of the Corps of Discovery were anxious to see the grizzly, and they got their chance on Saturday, October 20, 1804. As William Clark wrote in his journal, "Great number of Buffalow Elk & Deer, Goats. Our hunters killed 10 Deer & a Goat to day and wounded a white Bear, I saw several fresh tracks of those animals which is 3 times as large as a man track."

The following year, Meriwether Lewis wrote on May 5, 1805, of another encounter:

a most tremendious lookng anama, and extremely hard to kill notwithstanding he had five balls through his lungs and five others in various parts he swam more than half the distance across the river to a sandbar & it was at least twenty minutes before he died; [he] made the most tremendous roaring from the moment he was shot.

About a week later, Lewis noted in his diary that the curiosity of their party was pretty well satisfied with respect to this large bear.

While Lewis and Clark were making their journey across the continent to the Pacific, Zebulon Pike was sent to explore the source of the Mississippi River and then the southern plains. He captured two grizzly bear cubs, and in 1807, he took them east as gifts to President Thomas Jefferson.

Pike and the grizzly cubs arrived at the White House in November 1807. No one in the East, including Jefferson, had ever seen a grizzly bear. At Pike's suggestion, the two cubs were kept in a large cage in the north circle of the White House. Jefferson became fond of the grizzly cubs and wrote Charles Wilson Peale, who owned a museum in Baltimore, that he put them together in a ten-foot-square cage on the lawn in front of the White House. "For the first day they worried one another very much with play, but after that they played at times but were extremely happy together."

At one point, Jefferson separated the pair and put them in small cages, whereupon "one of the cubs became almost furious. I do not think they have any idea of hurting any one," wrote Jefferson, who later sent the two cubs to Peale's museum in Baltimore with the approach of winter in 1807.

On the plains, grizzly bears could be found stalking the vast buffalo herds looking for weak, sick, or old buffalo for meals. It was nature's way of helping to thin the countless number of buffalo roaming the plains.

The Blackfoot Indians told a story about a party of their warriors riding south one day to make war. As they approached a river crossing, one of the Indians, White Calf, thought he saw a human being high on a bluff, waiting to jump on a buffalo. Below, he saw buffalo passing under the bluff as they headed for water. The Blackfoot moved a little closer, sat down, and watched.

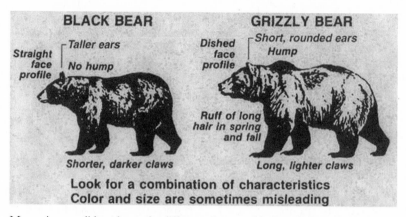

Many pioneers did not know the difference between black and grizzly bears. This illustration explains the difference. (Courtesy Wyoming Fish and Game)

Presently they saw a buffalo bull and a cow coming along the trail below the bluff. They were some distance behind the other buffalo. In a flash, a bear sprang on the cow and tried to drag her down. At her cry, the bull, which apparently had not seen the bear, charged in. Just then, the cow swung around with the bear on her back, making it impossible for the bull to attack.

A moment later, however, the bull's chance came. He caught the beast's stomach on his horns, tossed him high, caught him again, and tossed him again. When the bear struck the ground, he was battered and broken in the hindquarters. His entrails were hanging out. Slowly, however, he pulled himself up and fled the battlefield as the bull, apparently satisfied that the bear would offer no further trouble, walked off with the cow to water.

As westward settlement occurred and towns developed, local newspapers occasionally carried short items on bears in their neighborhood. The *Kinsley Graphic* in Kansas reported on May 31, 1879, that "Maj. Kirk captured a cub cinnamon bear [probably a black bear] near his camp last week. He took it to his home at Larned." It probably became too much to care for or it wandered away, because a few months later the *Larned Optic* on October 24 reported:

> For variety the south side is still ahead. Recently a large Cinnamon bear has been seen several times in the sand hills near the

bridge, and considerable excitement prevails among the residents. This is a fine chance for some of our gallant young bloods to get a good "hug." Go over and interview his bearship, gentlemen.

While grizzly bears were pretty much gone from the southern plains by the middle of the nineteenth century and from the northern plains by the late 1880s, black bear could still be found in some areas of the plains, especially in areas with trees along rivers and streams. From the earliest days of the white man on the plains, the black bear was hunted for its skins. In what is now eastern Oklahoma, A. P. Chouteau, a trader, shipped to New Orleans in 1824 the skins of three hundred female and one hundred cub black bears. The skins represented only one season's kill and suggest that black bear were then plentiful.

Another trader, Josiah Gregg, found black bear to be very common during the 1830s along the Canadian and Red Rivers. The same is true for black bears in Nebraska, where they ranged westward along the Niobrara and Loup rivers. Their Nebraska range may have also extended along other large rivers and into the Pine Ridge area. The last black bear killed in Nebraska was near Valentine in 1907. Today, however, black bears can still be found in eastern Oklahoma and occasionally in far southeast Kansas. In Texas, a few black bears exist in the Trans-Pecos region. Black bear occasionally have been seen on the plains of eastern Wyoming, in Montana, and in the western areas of North and South Dakota. On the western prairies and plains, however, there have been few reports of grizzly bears for many years.

Part V

THE FAMOUS AND THE OBSCURE

Fame is like a shaved pig with a greased tail, and it is only after it has slipped through the hands of some thousands, that some fellow, by mere chance holds on to it!
—Davy Crockett

30

The Day Chief Old Wolf Nearly Lost His Scalp

John L. Hatcher was a wiry little man, full of muscle and as fearless as any plains or mountain man in the Old West. He had red hair and piercing blue eyes. He was a good shot. He also was a good poker and euchre player.

Hatcher was born July 12, 1812, in Loudoun County, Virginia, where he grew up and received some education. As a young man, he left Virginia and joined a sister and her husband, who had settled at Wapakoneta, Ohio. When he arrived wearing a flashy suit of clothes, some local resident asked, "What's that?" Another replied, "That must be 'Dandy Jack from Caroline,'" which in the 1830s was the title of a popular song.

Hatcher found a job in a store, but did not like it, nor did he prosper. In 1835, he left Ohio and headed west to St. Louis, where he soon got a job with the Bent brothers. He joined their wagon train and traveled across the prairie and plains to Bent's Old Fort, located on the Arkansas River in what is now Colorado. Hatcher became a trapper, hunter, and trader for the Bents and made friends with such notables as Kit Carson. Hatcher made several trips for the company down the Chihuahua Trail into Mexico to buy and sell horses and mules. He also is known to have traveled as far as the North Platte River, and while opening trade with the Kiowa Indians, he was adopted into their tribe. He soon gained a reputation as an expert marksman, a good storyteller, and a diplomat without fear in his dealings with Indians, who called him "Freckled Hand."

In 1845, Hatcher and Caleb Greenwood, another Bent employee, accompanied Lieutenant James W. Abert's scientific expedition from Bent's Fort to the Canadian River. Hatcher assured the Comanches and Kiowas that Abert and his men were not hostile. After the Taos Rebellion in early 1847, Hatcher was among the volunteers recruited by William Bent to avenge the murder of his brother Charles, the territorial governor of New Mexico. Hatcher participated in the trial and hanging of the revolutionaries at Taos. He then served as a guide for two small military expeditions.

After nearly two decades in New Mexico, Hatcher and fifteen other men left Taos early in 1853 to drive a herd of cattle to Placerville, California, by way of Fort Laramie and South Pass. Hatcher returned east over the Gila Trail from Los Angeles, reaching New Mexico by December 1853. By spring of 1854, he entered the Santa Fe trade and in time enjoyed much success trading and freighting goods between Missouri and Santa Fe.

In the summer of 1857, Hatcher, then about forty-five years old, set out in early spring with a caravan of fifteen wagons and about as many men. Their destination was Westport, now part of Kansas City, Missouri.

Hatcher's men had been driving their wagons two abreast for protection. They were in Indian country, but as they approached Wagon Mound on the plains of northeastern New Mexico, Hatcher gave the order, and the wagons began to move in single file. On the open, rolling plains ahead, Hatcher knew that Indians, if there were any waiting, could be seen at a far distance.

The wagons had hardly had time to move into single file when suddenly a large band of Indians rode over a small rise in the ground and headed straight for the caravan. They were Comanches, but they were not attacking. The Indian chiefs—there were six or seven leading the warriors—were giving the peace sign.

Hatcher knew the ways of the Comanches, and he suspected they were coming to murder and rob. Hatcher, however, returned the sign of peace. He had little choice. Then he quickly gave the order to his men to corral their wagons in a circle and to stand by for trouble.

As the Indian chiefs came ahead of their braves, Hatcher saw that their leader was Old Wolf. The old Indian had been responsible for many raids on the southern plains. They had made Old Wolf's name a terror, especially among Mexicans traveling the Santa Fe Trail.

Hatcher cautiously welcomed Old Wolf and the other chiefs and invited them to have some refreshments. A blanket was thrown to the ground, and Hatcher seated himself beside Old Wolf. Sugar was served.

As Old Wolf and the other chiefs finished eating, Hatcher asked Old Wolf to send his young braves away, over the hill. The braves were standing beside their horses not far from the wagons. At this, Old Wolf and his chiefs stood up. So did Hatcher, who already sensed the old Indian's answer. Without waiting for a reply, Hatcher grabbed Old Wolf's hair with his left hand. With his right hand, Hatcher took his knife from its scabbard and held it to the chief's throat. "Send your braves over the hill now, or I'll kill you right where you are," demanded Hatcher.

Old Wolf shook his head.

"Send them on or I'll scalp you alive as you are!" said Hatcher in a firm voice.

Again, Old Wolf shook his head.

A second later, Hatcher began to carry out his threat, but he started slowly. Blood trickled from a tiny incision on Old Wolf's hairline down the Indian's forehead. Old Wolf quickly weakened. He ordered his next in command to send the young braves over the hill. The order was given, and the astonished braves quickly mounted their horses and rode away.

Still holding Old Wolf's hair, Hatcher ordered his men to unload their wagons. They did, piling bundles of pelts and furs inside the circle of wagons as a barricade. Then Hatcher's men climbed behind their barricade, passed out ammunition, and prepared for the battle they all knew was coming.

When Hatcher saw that his men were ready, he let go of Old Wolf's hair, gave the Indian a swift kick in the seat of his pants, and told the chiefs to leave. They did, and in haste. Hatcher quickly joined his men and prepared for an attack.

Thirty minutes passed, then an hour. The expected Indian attack still had not come as the sun began to set. Hatcher and his men remained on watch until dark, but there was no sign of Old Wolf and his band.

The night passed uneventfully. By dawn, there was still no sign of the Indians. Hatcher made the decision to move on. He gave the order, and the men reloaded their wagons. The caravan continued slowly toward the east and Westport. The remainder of the journey was peaceful. Not an Indian was seen.

Why Old Wolf and his band did not attack the wagon train is unknown. They outnumbered Hatcher and his men. It may have been that Old Wolf had lost face among his chiefs and braves, or that he had lost the element of surprise against Hatcher and his men.

Colonel Richard I. Dodge, plainsman and soldier, wrote in 1877, "As a rule, the Indian relies upon surprise, upon the effect of a sudden and furious dash . . . to demoralize his enemy and render him sure prey."

If surprise had been Old Wolf's aim, he had not succeeded. A more likely answer may have been Hatcher's bravery. His actions undoubtedly gained him sudden respect from Old Wolf. Comanches placed great importance on acts of bravery, and it was probably this sudden respect for Hatcher by Old Wolf and the other Indians that saved Hatcher and his men.

Later that summer, Hatcher returned to Santa Fe and made a trip over the trail the following year in 1858. Never once was he troubled by Indians.

Hatcher later moved to California, where he bought a large ranch and settled down. Still later he moved to Linn County, Oregon, where he died at the age of eighty-five in about 1898.

The fate of Old Wolf is not known, but early in the twentieth century, when the Santa Fe Railway tried to portray Indians in a way that promoted tourism in the West in 1927, they named one of ten new buffet-library-baggage cars built by Pullman-Standard for Old Wolf.

31

Two Letters from Abilene

It was late May 1909. The evening breeze rustled through the cottonwood trees along the banks of Mud Creek on the west edge of Abilene, Kansas. To the east, perhaps a mile, parents, relatives, and townspeople had filled Seelye's Theatre and were listening to the preliminaries of the high school graduation. Then the commencement speaker, Henry J. Allen, a Wichita newspaper editor, spoke.

One of the graduating seniors, a long-limbed and slender boy, listened as Allen expounded on the advantages of a college education. "I would sooner begin life over again with one arm cut off than attempt to struggle without a college education," concluded Allen.

The young man in the audience had already made up his mind to go to college, but he had only a sketchy notion of how he might get there. Then too, he really was not sure what he wanted to do in life.

The young man was Dwight David Eisenhower.

Within two years, young Eisenhower's desire for a college education would be realized. He would get a free education, the result of two letters he would write to a United States senator from Kansas. The career that would begin with those letters would later propel him from Abilene to the presidency of the United States.

Today, those original Eisenhower letters are guarded in the manuscript archives of the Kansas State Historical Society in Topeka, part of the collection of papers belonging to the late U.S. senator from

Kansas, Joseph L. Bristow. Photographic copies of the letters may be seen by visitors to the Eisenhower Museum in Abilene. Many years ago, the letters were valued at $3,500, but it is believed that they would bring at least ten times more today if sold on the open market.

When Dwight Eisenhower wrote the letters, he was a lean, lanky high school graduate, well liked among the young people of Abilene. He was active in sports, especially football. His schoolwork was about average, except in math, where he was considered a whiz. He could hold his own with his fists, and like many boys his age, he enjoyed hunting and fishing along the streams in Dickinson County.

Young Eisenhower's boyhood hero had been a tall man in his fifties, a fisherman, hunter, and guide named Bob Davis. He taught Ike how to use a flatboat, how to catch muskrat and mink, and how to hunt ducks with a shotgun.

It was from Bob Davis that young Eisenhower learned the fine art of poker. On camping trips, they played for matches, with Davis drumming percentages into Ike's head at every opportunity. Davis was illiterate, but he knew the percentages in poker, and he taught them to young Eisenhower. It may have been Davis's teaching of percentages that helped Ike in mathematics.

The summer after graduation, Dwight worked hard, as did his older brother, Edgar, who had graduated the year before. As Dwight recalled in 1967, "I changed from one job to another, depending upon the prospects for an extra dime an hour or an extra dollar a day. Because I did jump about, certain biographers have suggested that I was going through a period of indecision and had no idea what I wanted to do. The exact opposite was the truth. Ed and I had it all doped out."

Sometime in 1909, Dwight and Edgar had agreed to help each other go to college. Dwight would work to help send Edgar to college for a year. Then, if necessary, Edgar would drop out a year and help Dwight get started.

The fall of 1909, Edgar went to the University of Michigan at Ann Arbor, and Dwight went to work at the Belle Springs Creamery in Abilene. By the end of the school year, he had sent Edgar more than two hundred dollars to help with his education.

Dwight also had changed. He had filled out; his chest was larger, and his arms had muscles like iron. No longer was he a string bean.

In the summer of 1910, Edgar returned home for vacation and got a job to earn money for his schooling. That summer, Dwight became night engineer—the foreman—at the creamery, a job that paid ninety dollars a month, and he became close friends with Everett J. "Swede" Hazlett, a boy from the north side of town. Hazlett was a year younger than Dwight.

Swede Hazlett had spent three years in a military school in Wisconsin. He had wanted an appointment to West Point but instead received one to Annapolis. At Annapolis, however, Hazlett had failed mathematics in the entrance exam. Hazlett's congressman arranged for him to take the exam again, and in the summer of 1910, while managing a small office of a manufacturing firm in Abilene, he was cramming for his second try.

Evenings after work, Hazlett would visit Dwight at the creamery, where the two sometimes played penny-ante poker into the early morning. Dwight's shift was from 6 P.M. to 6 A.M. Hazlett talked to Dwight with enthusiasm about the naval academy. For a time, young Eisenhower listened only politely, but gradually, he became genuinely interested in the service school. For one thing, it offered a free education. For another, it provided a career.

From Hazlett, Eisenhower learned that appointments were also made to Annapolis by U.S. senators, not just by members of the House of Representatives. Even though young Ike felt his chances were slim, he thought he would give it a try. On August 20, 1910, he wrote the first of several letters to Senator Joseph Bristow at nearby Salina, Kansas. It read:

Dear Senator:
    I would very much like to enter either the school at Annapolis or the one at West Point. In order to do this I must have an appointment to one of these places and so I am writing you to secure the same.
    I have graduated from high school and will be 19 years of age this fall.
    If you find it possible to appoint me to one of these schools, your kindness with certainly be appreciated by me. Trusting to hear from you concerning this matter at your earliest convenience.
Respectfully yours,
Dwight Eisenhower

This photograph, worn by time, was taken during Dwight Eisenhower's high school days. The future president is on the right. This photograph was apparently taken on one of young Eisenhower's camping trips near Abilene. Others are not identified. (Courtesy Kansas State Historical Society)

Interestingly, Eisenhower was already nineteen years old, not eighteen, as he indicated in his letter. This may have been because in 1910, candidates for Annapolis had to be not under sixteen nor over twenty at the date of the entrance examination, which would be the third Tuesday in April 1911. The rule read: "A candidate is ineligible for examination on the day he becomes 20 years of age." On the day of the examination, young Eisenhower would be twenty years old and therefore unable to qualify for Annapolis.

Three days after Dwight sent the letter, he received a reply from Senator Bristow's secretary at Salina. It informed him that the senator was out of town but that Eisenhower's application had been filed, along with others the senator already had.

Ike then sought the help of influential persons in Abilene. Letters were written to Senator Bristow by Charles Harger, publisher of the town's newspaper; P. W. Heath, another Abilene newspaper publisher and former postmaster; and J. B. Chase, an Abilene merchant.

For two weeks, young Eisenhower heard nothing further from Senator Bristow. During that time, he read in the newspapers that competitive examinations for the senator's appointment would be held in October. Impatient, he wrote a second letter to Bristow on September 3, 1910.

> Dear Sir:
> Sometime ago I wrote to you applying for an appointment to West Point or Annapolis. As yet I have heard nothing definite from you about the matter, but I noticed in the daily papers that you would soon give a competitive examination for these appointments.
> Now, if you find it impossible to give me an appointment outright, to one of these places, would I have the right to enter this competitive examination?
> If so, will you please explain the conditions to be met in entering this examination, and the studies to be covered. Trusting to hear from you at your earliest convenience, I am,
> Respectfully yours,
> Dwight Eisenhower
> Abilene, Kansas

If young Eisenhower had already been on Senator Bristow's list, it is doubtful that the senator would have replied so quickly to Eisenhower's second letter. It brought an almost immediate reply. The senator said there were vacancies for both service schools, and he authorized Eisenhower to appear at the office of the Kansas State Superintendent of Public Instruction at Topeka, October 4 and 5, to take the competitive exam prepared by the War Department.

Eisenhower sought out Swede Hazlett, who had been studying for the same type of exam all summer. Hazlett, as he recalled years later, "was well up in the methods and short cuts of the cram school."

"Every afternoon at about 2 Ike would come to my office and we would work until about 5," recalled Hazlett. "During these 3-hour periods I managed to sandwich in enough office work to keep my job, but not much more. Ike's God-given brain sped him along and soon he was way ahead of his self-appointed teacher."

Eisenhower took the two-day exam in the Topeka office of Edward T. Fairchild, state superintendent of schools, and returned to Abilene. "He returned confident he had done his best," remembered Hazlett, adding, "but none too confident of the outcome. That's another trait of his—he always puts forth his best efforts, but never underrates the opposition."

U.S. Senator Joseph L. Bristow of Salina, Kansas. Young Dwight Eisenhower applied to Bristow for an appointment to a military academy. (Courtesy Kansas State Historical Society)

Eisenhower did well on the exam. On file in the Kansas State Historical Society archives at Topeka, among Senator Bristow's papers, is the record of the grades made by the eight young men who took the exam. The typewritten page contains notes written in longhand by Senator Bristow.

Dwight "Eisenhour," as the name was spelled, stood second among the eight. He was the highest of the four men wanting Annapolis, second to those wanting West Point. His grade average was $87\frac{1}{2}$ out of a possible 100. "Eisenhour" apparently decided at the last minute to give himself all possible chance of success. He is listed as an "either," as one of the four young men who would accept either Annapolis or West Point.

The only young man who scored more than Eisenhower was George Pulsifer, the son of a retired U.S. Army sergeant at Fort Leavenworth, Kansas. Pulsifer scored $89\frac{2}{8}$, and he wanted West Point.

Dwight David Eisenhower as he
appeared about 1910. (Courtesy
Kansas State Historical Society)

But as Pulsifer explained later, he obtained an "at large" appointment
from the president through a general officer under whom his father
had served. This meant young Eisenhower was at the top of Senator
Bristow's list.

Interestingly, Eisenhower's lowest score was in United States history. He received a 73.

It was nearly three weeks after Ike took the exam at Topeka that
he learned he had been selected for West Point. In late October 1910,
he received a letter from Senator Bristow:

> My dear Mr. Eisenhower:
> I have decided to send in your name to the Secretary of War
> as my nominee for the vacancy in the West Point Military Academy occurring next spring. The entrance examination will be
> held at Jefferson Barracks, Mo., on the second Tuesday in January. Detailed instruction as to when and where to report will
> doubtless be sent you by the War Department.
> The form of nomination blank furnished me by the Department calls for a statement of your exact age, years and months,
> and a statement as to how long you have been an actual resident

Dwight Eisenhower's original first letter to Kansas Senator Joseph Bristow, August 20, 1910. The original is in the Bristow Collection, Kansas State Historical Society at Topeka.

of Kansas. Please send me this information at once, so that I may send in the formal nomination without delay.
With best wishes, I am
Very Truly yours
Joseph Bristow

The afternoon Dwight Eisenhower received the letter, he hurried to see Swede Hazlett, who later recalled that the appointment to West Point "was a cruel blow, and Ike didn't like it any better than I did. All his hopes had been aimed at Annapolis and he felt that, through me, he knew a good deal about it. I urged him to write the senator and tell him that he greatly preferred the Navy, and beg a reconsideration. He muttered something about 'not looking any gift horse in the mouth.'"

Eisenhower did not ask Senator Bristow to reconsider. As Ike recalled in 1967, "Even before the results of the examination were published, I learned that I would be barred from going to Annapolis.

Dwight Eisenhower's original second letter to Kansas Senator Joseph Bristow of Salina, Kansas. The letter is dated September 3, 1910. The original is in the Bristow Collection, Kansas State Historical Society at Topeka.

The entrance regulations for that academy specified an age from 16 to 20, but Swede and I had earlier assumed that the maximum applied until the 21st birthday had been reached. After taking the first examination, I learned that because I would be almost 21 by the time the next class enlisted, I was ineligible for entrance to the Naval Academy." Late that afternoon, Ike replied to Senator Bristow's letter:

> Dear Sir:
>   Your letter of the 24th instant has just been received. I wish to thank you sincerely for the favor you have shown me in appointing me to West Point.
>   In regard to the information desired, I am just 19 years and 11 days of age, and have been a resident of Abilene, Kan. for eighteen years.
>   Thanking you again, I am
> Very truly yours,
> Dwight Eisenhower

Again young Eisenhower gave an incorrect age, even though he actually qualified for West Point because the requirements were different from Annapolis. In 1919, candidates for West Point could not be under seventeen nor over twenty-two as of March 1, 1911. On that date, Eisenhower would be twenty-one years old and would quality.

In 1952, *Life* magazine queried Eisenhower about the age discrepancy in the letters in order to answer a letter from a reader. Ike's answering cable said: "I was born 14 October 1890, as recorded in the family Bible. I have no recollection of the letter you quoted, but I remember clearly that sometime late in 1910 or early 1911 I personally informed Senator Bristow that, having just learned of Naval Academy age regulations, I withdrew my application for appointment to the institution because of overage." There is no correspondence of this nature in the collection of Bristow's papers at the Kansas State Historical society, but it is likely that Eisenhower gave him the message orally.

Ike took the West Point examination at Jefferson Barracks near St. Louis in January 1911. He passed somewhat above the middle of all those admitted and received orders to report to West Point on June 14, 1911.

A few days before he was to report, young Eisenhower was ready to leave Abilene. His train was due shortly. He came downstairs with his bag, and his mother and brother, Milton, were waiting for him on the side porch. Ike had said good-bye to everyone but them. The soldier-to-be put down his bag and bent to pet his dog, Flip. Then he straightened up and looked at his mother. She told him to take care of himself and to be a good boy. He said he would. Then, for the first time in the presence of her sons, she cried.

Dwight tried to comfort her, but not being very successful, he turned to Milton and told him to "look after Mother." At that, Milton began to cry.

Dwight did the only thing a boy from the south side could do. He ordered his dog to stay home, picked up his bag, and almost ran to the street. He headed north, toward the railroad station. There was one last good-bye over the shoulder as the whistle of an approaching train could be heard in the distance.

A few days later, Dwight David Eisenhower reported to the United States military academy at West Point and began his career as a military man—a career that eventually took him to the White House.

32

Spotted Tail's Daughter

It was a cold February morning in 1866 when Spotted Tail (Sinte Galeska or Sinte Gleska in Lakota), a Brule Sioux chief, led a party of his principal warriors and a number of Indian women from a camp on the icy Powder River and began a journey south to Fort Laramie, two hundred sixty miles away. It was winter, and the trail they followed took them through rough snow-covered mountainous country that was frozen and bleak. It was a sad journey because they were taking the body of Spotted Tail's daughter to Fort Laramie, where she wanted to be laid to rest.

Spotted Tail was born in 1823 on the White River west of the Missouri River in what is now South Dakota. He grew up watching his people, the Sioux, battle the Pawnee for hunting grounds on the plains. By the time he was thirty, Spotted Tail was a Shirt Wearer, or protector of all people in his tribe. His shirt, according to one account, was adorned with more than one hundred locks of hair, each representing coups, scalps taken, and horses captured from the Pawnee. By then his wife had given birth to a daughter, but exactly when and where she was born has been lost in time.

Spotted Tail's daughter was named Ah-Ho-Ap-Pa, which in translation means "wheat flour." She also was known as Mni Akuwin, meaning "Brings Water Home Woman." Little else is known of her early years until after an incident occurred late in 1854 about eight

Spotted Tail, chief of the Brule Sioux (1823–1881). He was an outspoken advocate for the rights of his people. (Courtesy Speck-Choute Photographic Collection, American Philosophical Society)

miles east of Fort Laramie on the Oregon Trail. A company of Mormons was passing a Brule Sioux Indian camp when a lame cow belonging to the Mormons ran into the Indian camp. The Indians were out of government provisions. An Indian shot the cow, skinned it, and cooked it for the hungry Indians. The incident was reported at Fort Laramie, and Lieutenant J. L. Grattan, along with twenty-seven soldiers plus a drunken interpreter, went to the Indian camp to arrest the thief. The Indian who shot the animal refused to surrender. Grattan, who later was described as arrogant, ordered his men to fire one volley at the Indians. Led by Spotted Tail, the Indians suddenly turned on the soldiers, killing Lieutenant Gratton and all but one of the soldiers, who apparently later died of his injuries. Other nearby Indians joined in the uprising and soon raided a trading post operated by the American Fur Company three miles upriver of Fort Laramie. The Indians took everything and fled. There were not enough soldiers at Fort Laramie to pursue the Indians.

Within weeks, six hundred soldiers under the command of General William S. Harney were searching for Spotted Tail and his band.

Early in 1855, the soldiers found them at Ash Hollow and tried to capture them. In what is called the battle of Bluewater Creek, Spotted Tail was wounded but escaped. Eighty-six Sioux were killed and about seventy others taken prisoner, including Spotted Tail's wife and baby daughter, Ah-Ho-Ap-Pa, who were taken to Fort Laramie, where they lived in what the soldiers called "squaw-camp" for more than two years.

Meanwhile, the army sent word that the hostile Indians must surrender. In October 1855, Spotted Tail and four other Sioux surrendered at Fort Laramie and were taken to Fort Leavenworth, Kansas Territory, and later moved to Fort Kearny, Nebraska Territory. About a year later, they were released. Spotted Tail's experiences as a prisoner changed him. He began to realize the power and number of whites and that an Indian victory over them was highly improbable. He also began to realize that to gain peace for his people, they would have to submit to the wishes of the whites—but he also learned the art of negotiation through talking.

When Spotted Tail was released by the U.S. Army, he returned to his people and was reunited with his wife and daughter. He retained his status of Shirt Wearer, but there was now peace between the Sioux and whites. Occasionally Spotted Tail would bring his wife and daughter to visit Fort Laramie. We know something about their visits because Eugene Fitch Ware, an officer at Fort Laramie, was there and later wrote about them. Ware noted that during the daytime, Ah-Ho-Ap-Pa "came to the sutler's store and sat on a bench outside, near the door, watching as if she were living on the sights she saw. She was particularly fond of witnessing guard-mount in the morning and dress-parade in the evening. Whoever officiated principally on these occasions put on a few extra touches for her specific benefit, at the suggestion of Major Wood, the Post Commander. The Officer-of-the-guard always appeared in an eighteen-dollar red silk sash, ostrich plume, shoulder-straps, and about two hundred dollars' worth of astonishing raiment, such as, in the field, we boys used to look upon with loathing and contempt. We all knew her by sight, but she never spoke to any of us."

Ware wrote that among the officers at Fort Laramie Ah-Ho-Ap-Pa was called "the princess." Ware observed that "she was looking always looking, as if she were feeding upon what she saw. Her manner of action was known to all, and was frequently referred to as an Indian girl of great dignity. Some thought she was acting vain, and some thought that she did not know or comprehend her own manner. There was no silly curiosity in her demeanor. She saw everything, but asked no questions. She expressed no surprise, and exhibited not a particle of emotion. She only gazed intently."

In his conversations with other officers at Fort Laramie, Ware also learned that Spotted Tail had been offered as many as two hundred ponies for his daughter, but he had refused because she did not want to marry an Indian. She wanted to marry an army officer and supposedly had said she would not marry anybody but a *capitan,* a Spanish word the Indians used to identify any officer with shoulder straps. Ware also was told that as a teenager, Ah-Ho-Ap-Pa was "as strong as a mule" and almost always carried a knife.

Once a Blackfoot soldier running with her father's band tried to carry her off, but she fought and cut him almost to pieces. She also tried to learn to read and speak English from a captured white boy, but the boy escaped. Ware was also told that she carried around with her "a little bit of a red book, with a gold cross printed on it, that General Harney gave her mother many years ago." She carried it in a piece of dressed rawhide. Ah-Ho-Ap-Pa told her father and her people that they were fools for not making peace and living in houses.

Ware also recounted a story he heard about the time Spotted Tail took his daughter with him to visit Jack Morrow, a former government teamster, who built a trading ranch about twelve miles west of Cottonwood Springs in modern Lincoln County, Nebraska:

> She was treated in fine style, and ate a bushel of candy and sardines, but her father was insulted by some drunken fellow and went away boiling mad. When he got home to his tepee he said he never would go around any more where they were white men, except to kill them. She and her father got into a regular quarrel over it, and she pulled out her knife and began cutting herself across the arms and ribs, and in a minute she was bleeding in about forty places, and said that if he didn't say different she was going to kill herself. He knocked her down as cold as a wedge, and had her cuts fixed up by the squaws with pine pitch; and when she came to he promised her that she could go, whenever he did, to see the whites.

For Ah-Ho-Ap-Pa and her family, there was relative calm in their lives until late 1864, when Colonel John Chivington and seven hundred Colorado volunteers swept down on Black Kettle's camp on Sand Creek in eastern Colorado, killing at least one hundred fifty Indians. Black Kettle, a Cheyenne chief who a few weeks earlier in a meeting with the governor of Colorado had agreed to live in peace, escaped and spread the news of the massacre. Indians throughout the region decided to unite and fight. Spotted Tail was pulled into an intertribal alliance with the Cheyennes, Arapahos, and three other Sioux bands. Among the Indians' retaliation for the Sand Creek raid, Spotted Tail led an attack on Julesburg, a stage station in western Nebraska, in January 1865.

When Spotted Tail returned to his family in camp on the Powder River in February, he found his daughter ill. She was suffering from tuberculosis and was living in a chilly and lonesome tepee among the pines on the west bank of the Powder River. She had not seen a white person since she left Fort Laramie in August 1864. Near death, she told her father that she was ready to die and wanted to be buried in the cemetery at Fort Laramie, "where the soldiers were buried, up on the hill, near the grave of 'Old Smoke,'" a distant relative and a great chief among the Sioux in former years.

When she died, there were great lamentations among her people. The skin of a freshly killed deer was held over the fire and thoroughly permeated and creosoted with smoke. Her body was wrapped in it, and it was tightly bound around her with thongs so that she was temporarily embalmed. Her father sent a runner to announce that he was coming to Fort Laramie to bury his daughter.

Two of her white ponies were tied together, side by side, and her body was placed across their backs. Her father, a party of principal warriors, and a number of women then started for Fort Laramie. The journey took fifteen days. When the Indians camped each evening, cottonwood and willow trees were cut down so that their ponies could eat the tops and gnaw the wood and bark.

When Spotted Tail's large party got within fifteen miles of Fort Laramie, a runner was sent ahead to inform Colonel Maynadier that they were near. In consultation with other officers, Colonel Maynadier ordered an ambulance dispatched, guarded by a company of cavalry in full uniform, followed by two twelve-pound mountain howitzers, with posit lions in red chevrons. When the soldiers reached the Indians, the body was placed in the ambulance. Behind it were led the girl's two white ponies.

When the soldiers and Indians reached the Laramie River, a couple of miles from the post, the garrison turned out. With Colonel Maynadier at the head, they met and escorted the Indians to the post where they were assigned quarters. The next day, a scaffold was erected near the grave of "Old Smoke." It was made of tent poles twelve feet long embedded in the ground and fastened with thongs over which a buffalo robe was laid, and on which the coffin was to be placed. The Indians killed the two white ponies, and their heads and tails were nailed to the poles of the scaffold so that Ah-Ho-Ap-Pa could ride through the fair hunting grounds of the skies.

The coffin that was made was lavishly decorated. The body was not unbound from its deerskin shroud, but was wrapped in a bright red blanket and placed in the coffin, which was mounted on the wheels of an artillery caisson. After the coffin came a twelve-pound howitzer, and the procession started for the cemetery with the entire garrison in full uniform. Although still cold, the weather had moderated somewhat. The Reverend Mr. Wright, the post chaplain, suggested an elaborate burial service. Spotted Tail was consulted. He wanted his daughter buried in the Indian fashion, so that she would go not where the white people went, but where the red people went. Spotted Tail's every request was followed by the colonel. Spotted Tail gave the chaplain the parfleche his daughter had carried, which contained the little book that General Harney had given to her mother many years before. It was a small Episcopal prayer book, such as was used in the regular army. Spotted Tail's wife could not read it, but she considered it a talisman. The chaplain placed the prayer book in the coffin. Then Colonel Maynadier stepped forward and deposited a pair of white cavalry gloves in the coffin to keep her hands warm while she was making the journey. Another officer added a crisp one-dollar bill so she might buy what she wanted on the journey.

Each of the Indian women then came up, one at a time, and talked quietly to Ah-Ho-Ap-Pa, and each put a remembrance in the coffin. One placed a small looking glass, another a string of colored beads, and another a pinecone. The lid was then closed and fastened. Indian women lifted the coffin and placed it on the scaffold. A fresh

As was Indian custom, Spotted Tail's daughter was laid to rest above ground. This photograph, taken several years after her death, shows Fort Laramie in the background. (Courtesy Wyoming Historical Department)

buffalo skin was laid over the coffin and bound down to the sides of the scaffold with thongs. On command, soldiers facing away from the coffin discharged three volleys in rapid succession. The soldiers and the Indians then returned to the post, but the howitzer squad remained. They built a large fire of pine wood and fired the gun every half-hour all night until daybreak.

Eugene Fitch Ware perhaps summarized Ah-Ho-Ap-Pa's life when he wrote that she "wanted to find somebody to love worth loving. Her soul bled to death. Like an epidendrum, she was feeding upon the air."

33

The Nebraska Hoax King

Early newspaper men (and perhaps a handful of newspaper women) on the prairies and plains often stretched the truth to brighten what otherwise would have been dull and mundane local news. One such journalist was John G. Maher, who did more than stretch the truth. He wanted his creations to be believed, and to do so, he provided physical evidence to make them believable.

Maher grew up in Nebraska, where his father was a state senator during the late 1880s. After young Maher completed his education at Fremont, Nebraska, he taught school for a few years and then went to work for the government, first in the mail service, and then operating a government land office at Chadron near the sand hill region of northern Nebraska. He studied law and was admitted to the bar just before the Ghost Dance phenomenon occurred in northwest Nebraska on the Sioux Indian reservation.

When that occurred, Maher went to view it, along with U.S. troops, as a special correspondent of James Gordon Bennett's New York *Herald*. Afterward, he continued to send stories to the *Herald*.

Whether Maher had read Mark Twain's story about a petrified man is not known, but after Maher learned that an eastern archaeologist had found dinosaur remains "a million years old" somewhere in the West, and the story attracted much national attention, he got the idea of planting an "ossified man" for scientists to find.

188

During the summer of 1892, Maher and some cronies made a plaster cast of a large black soldier from the Ninth Cavalry at nearby Fort Robinson, poured concrete into the cast, and created a stonelike figure of a man. Maher even used shingles to flatten the figure's feet because he had read that prehistoric men were flat-footed.

In secret, Maher and his conspirators hauled the concrete figure by wagon to near where some local scientific buffs were digging for fossils, and buried it in some clay.

On a rainy Sunday morning some days later, the buffs discovered the figure half-uncovered in some clay. Astounded, they declared it an ossified man and on the spot classified him prehistoric. Four days after the figure was uncovered, the *Dawes County Journal* at Chadron reported the find and noted:

> The two Rossiter brothers were collecting fossils about 3 miles from town in a strip of bad lands at the Natural Wall when Ed discovered what he at first thought to be a bone projecting from a bank of clay. A little digging brought him to what he found to be the hand of a man. He called his brother Clyde to watch the treasure while he came to the city for help. That evening the valuable find was safe at the Rossiter hotel and after the clay was partially removed from the body it was placed on exhibition. . . . The face resembles that of a Negro . . . but his shapely heels indicate Caucasian blood. . . . The medical fraternity and all others who have seen the specimen laugh at the idea that it is not genuine. It is undoubtedly the most perfect specimen of the kind ever discovered, and is worth many thousands of dollars. Mr. Rossiter intends taking it to the Chicago World Fair.

Naturally Maher, as western correspondent for the New York *Herald,* sent dispatches about the find to the paper. His stories were welcomed and given wide coverage.

Another time Maher and some friends decided to stop people in Chadron from going to Thermopolis, Wyoming, or Hot Springs, South Dakota, for the alleged cures offered by the boiling natural springs. Maher thought people ought to remain in Chadron, which had two boiling springs near town.

Maher and his cronies sank sacks of soda to the bottom of the Chadron springs and then promoted them. By the time people came to try the water, Maher had already made up testimonies from people who had drunk from the springs and thrown away their crutches.

In the 1930s, Maher created another hoax by sending stories to the New York *Herald* reporting a gigantic monster living in Lake Walgren near Hay Springs in Sheridan County, Nebraska. Other papers in the East picked them up. Even the London *Times* ran a story about the monster, which was described as having a head "like an oil barrel shiny black in the moonlight. . . . Its flashing green eyes spit fire. . . . When it roars and flips its powerful tail the farmers are made seasick. . . . It eats a dozen calves when it comes ashore. . . . It flattens the cornfields. . . . The gnashing of its teeth sounds like a clap of thunder."

Maher's hoaxes ended when he died in 1939 at the age of seventy. Today, when his name is occasionally mentioned by old-timers in western Nebraska, there are smiles on their faces as they remember that easterners believed the far-fetched tales as told by one of their own.

34

Fort Mann's Woman Soldier

It was in October 1847 when First Lieutenant Amandus Schnabel set out from Fort Leavenworth with infantry Company D of the newly formed Battalion of Missouri Volunteers, bound for Fort Mann, located on the north bank of the Arkansas River a few miles west of modern-day Dodge City, Kansas. In Schnabel's company was a private called Bill Newcomb, who joined the company just before its departure from Fort Leavenworth. Newcomb, however, was really a young woman.

More than two months earlier, the War Department in Washington, D.C., authorized the governor of Missouri to recruit and outfit a detachment of soldiers to restore peace along the Santa Fe Trail in the upper Arkansas River area. Lieutenant Colonel William Gilpin, who had fought in the Mexican War, was appointed commander.

Little is known about the soldiers' journey from Fort Leavenworth to Fort Mann, other than it took the troops about a month to reach Fort Mann. Traveling with Company D were two other companies, one infantry, the other artillery. Two weeks earlier, Gilpin and two companies of cavalry made up of Missouri volunteers had left Fort Leavenworth for Fort Mann.

Construction of Fort Mann had begun less than two years earlier, when the U.S. Army quartermaster department hired forty teamsters to build the post. It was not intended to be a regular army post

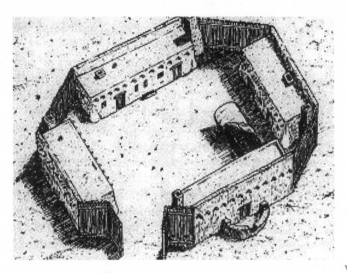

A bird's-eye view drawing of Fort Mann, Kansas, about 1846 or
1847. (Author's Collection)

but rather a depot located an equal distance between Fort Leavenworth and Santa Fe, where wagon trains and travelers could repair
their wagons and get supplies. One account describes the post as rect-
angular in shape with a diameter of sixty feet, consisting of a tall
wooden stockyard with two one-foot-thick gates. Inside were four log
and sod buildings. At least, that was the plan when Daniel P. Mann,
about thirty-five years old and a master teamster, was hired in 1846
by the U.S. Army quartermaster department to oversee the post,
which soon was called Fort Mann.

The location of the post, however, was in the heart of Pawnee
and Comanche country. Soon after the construction began, a teamster went fishing in the Arkansas River only a hundred yards away. He
was ambushed by Comanches, lanced, shot, and scalped within view
of the other teamsters working at the post. A couple days later, Indians stole fifteen yoke of oxen and forty head of mules.

The Indian threat soon caused most of the teamsters to pack up
and leave east over the Santa Fe Trail, but Captain A. W. Enos of the
quartermaster department convinced about ten teamsters to remain
and complete the construction work by promising to pay each of
them thirty dollars a month instead of the usual twenty. Enos then

convinced a passing Indian trader, John Simpson "Blackfoot" Smith, to take command of the small band of teamsters. Smith was a veteran mountain man and Indian trader who was married to a Southern Cheyenne woman. It did not take Smith long to realize that Mann was a "prairie prison." His only claim to fame as commander of Fort Mann is that he signed up one more man from a passing wagon train to work at the post. Only seven days after Smith took command, he quit and joined a wagon train going east, claiming that the teamsters at the post probably would lose their scalps to the Comanche.

Smith gave command to Thomas Sloan, the blacksmith, but progress in completing the buildings inside the stockade was slow. The teamsters were afraid to leave the safety of the stockade for fear of Indians. The only times they left the post to cut lumber was when large wagon trains with many armed men paused at the post and offered protection. On June 19, 1847, the teamsters' fears were realized when four hundred Indians tried to capture the post. Sloan and his small band repelled several attacks and killed fifteen Indians and wounded thirty or forty more with their rifles and a six-pound canon. But during a lull in the fighting, three teamsters left the safety of the stockade, only to be killed and scalped. Sloan realized it was time to abandon the post. After the Indians withdrew, he and his men hitched up the cannon and headed for Santa Fe, deserting Fort Mann.

When Indians learned that Fort Mann had been abandoned, they increased hostilities along the upper Arkansas. Reports suggest that forty-seven Americans were killed, thirty-three wagons were destroyed, and more than 6,500 animals were stolen from travelers along the Santa Fe Trail that summer of 1847. It was then that the Battalion of Missouri Volunteers was organized and outfitted in Missouri. Lieutenant Colonel William Gilpin was made their commander and was ordered to protect travelers and restore peace. Gilpin directed one artillery company and two companies of infantry to repair and enlarge Fort Mann. Meanwhile, he took the two companies of cavalry to Big Timbers in what is now Colorado.

When the three companies, including the one with First Lieutenant Amandus Schnabel and Private Bill Newcomb, reached Fort Mann, the formerly deserted post suddenly had a population of two hundred seventy, including fifty-four officers and two hundred sixteen soldiers. There was hardly room to quarter even one-fifth of the troops in the buildings, so tents were set up in the open area of the stockade. The little post was suddenly crowded and dirty. The motley force of mostly inexperienced soldiers within the stockade were all volunteers, and most had never before been on the plains, let alone fought Indians. Two companies were made up of Germans from St. Louis who spoke little English. The remaining company was composed of English-speaking men.

Some days later, a well-meaning attempt to entertain a party of wandering Indians ended in the killing of nine Pawnee and the wounding of two others. As winter set in, morale among the volunteers was low. Officers were abused, and insubordination was commonplace. When one volunteer sent a letter east in early December 1847, he described the post as "the most desolate and uninteresting place upon the face of the earth." It was. Vermin infested the camp and made living conditions very bad.

But for one officer, life at Fort Mann was often enjoyable. The previous September, First Lieutenant Schnabel made plans to enjoy his campaign on the plains. He convinced a young woman named Caroline Newcomb to dress as a man and enlist as a private in his company under the name Bill Newcomb. She did. Schnabel disguised Caroline in soldier's clothing and had her report under the name Bill whenever she stood in formation. When the volunteers came west with the troops from Fort Leavenworth, Private Bill Newcomb was with them. Because the volunteers at Fort Mann numbered two hundred seventy persons, the buildings could not house everyone. Tents were set up on the ground inside the stockade, and Lieutenant Schnabel occupied one of these, which he shared with Private Bill (Caroline) Schnabel.

Whether or not some of the volunteers knew that Bill was really a woman is not known, but by December 1847, Lieutenant Schnabel was urging Bill to desert and return to Missouri because she was pregnant. She successfully fled the post and joined a wagon train bound for Missouri, but by then, the officers over Schnabel had learned what had happened.

Lieutenant Schnabel was arrested and taken to Bent's Fort, where in early January 1848 his court-martial was held. He was accused of resorting "to various means to keep the said female disguised as a male, off from duty in the Company under different pretexts and during all or portions of that period was tenting, sleeping and cohabiting with the said female, thereby defrauding the United States of the service of a good and competent soldier."

Schnabel was later discharged from the service and apparently went east. Whether he returned to Caroline Newcomb is not known, but marriage records in St. Louis tell of the marriage of Amandus V. Schnabel to one Martha A. Stewart on January 6, 1856.

35

The Legend of Rawhide

Although the word *rawhide* was used in England as early as 1561, it did not come into use in the United States until the nineteenth century. One legend suggests French Canadian mountain men in the Rocky Mountains translated the French word *parfleche*, meaning untanned leather, to "rawhide" in describing dressed-out beaver pelts. They also made containers, moccasins, soles for shoes, and a sort of suitcase usually decorated with painted designs from rawhide.

Another legend with more detail is set in 1849, when thousands of people were following the Oregon Trail west to the California goldfields. Tradition has it that in one party of Forty-Niners was a young man from Pike County, Missouri. When the party started west, he boasted that he was going to shoot the first Indian he saw. Others in the party thought he was full of hot air, and during the party's first month of travel across what is now northeast Kansas into Nebraska, the young man apparently forgot what he had boasted about doing. Others in the party had not.

When their wagons reached eastern Wyoming in early June 1949 and what is today Niobrara County, someone called the young man's attention to a camp of a few Indians on the Platte River and apparently joked about him killing an Indian. To everyone's surprise, as they neared the Indian village, the young man shot a defenseless Indian woman.

The Indians were furious. When the party of Forty-Niners camped a few miles down the trail at midday, Indian warriors with reinforcements surrounded their camp and demanded that they be given the man who shot the Indian woman. Whether the emigrants turned over the young man or he gave himself up is not clear, but he was soon in the hands of the angry Indians, who tied him to a wagon wheel and proceeded to skin him alive. According to the tale, which was told and retold countless times, the poor chap fainted a number of times but lived till they had him nearly skinned in front of the eyes of the emigrants, including the young man's mother. She reportedly died a few days later, as the emigrants continued their journey west.

The legend claims that this is how the word *rawhide* made its first appearance in the West and how Rawhide Creek and Rawhide Buttes in Niobrara County, Wyoming, got their names. A story handed down by Sioux Indians, however, suggests that Rawhide Buttes got its name in a different way. The Sioux legend tells how some of their people killed a great many buffalo, skinned them, and left a great pile of raw, green hides at the foot of one of the buttes that dotted the landscape. When the Sioux returned, the rawhides were gone, apparently stolen by white trappers. It was then, according to legend, that the Sioux gave the buttes the name Tahalo Paha—*Tahalo* meaning "rawhide," and *Paha* meaning "hills" or "buttes"—to remind them of what happened.

Whether or not there is any truth to the legend, the citizens of Niobrara County since 1949 have annually held a Legend of Rawhide pageant reenacting the legend with a wagon train, the death of an Indian woman, and the skinning alive of the white man. Even if the legend is not true, it has long since become part of the history of Niobrara County, which was created in 1911 and organized in 1913 in the tallgrass prairie of eastern Wyoming.

During the nineteenth century, the word *rawhide* came to be used in other ways. For instance, in the 1870s small cattlemen who failed to settle down were often referred to as "rawhiders." The word *rawhide* was also used to describe a cowboy who was good with a branding iron.

Because rawhide was tough and frequently used to make door hinges, springs, ropes, and clothing and to repair just about anything, it was nicknamed "Mexican iron." When the Mormons traveled overland to Utah, they often used rawhide for repairing wheel spokes, gun stocks, and many other things. It was then that rawhide was sometimes called "Mormon iron."

Rawhide was also used in combination with other words to suggest difficult tasks and things. For instance, slabs of lumber with the bark left on was called "rawhide lumber," and a "rawhide outfit" was a tough group to work for. Rawhide is also another name for a whip braided from the same material.

36

Black Mary

Many characters in the Old West became well known. The stories of some were embellished in dime novels and newspaper reports, which created heroes and almost mythical figures who are now legends. Mary Fields, also known as Black Mary and Stagecoach Mary, never gained such fame outside of the region around Cascade, a farming and ranching community on the rolling prairie of central Montana.

Mary Fields was not a westerner by birth. She was born a slave on a plantation in Hickman County, Tennessee, in 1832 during the presidency of Andy Jackson. She grew up an orphan, never received a formal education, lived by her wits and her strength, never married, and had no children.

As a child, she was a playmate and friend of the plantation owner's daughter, Dolly, who became a Catholic nun in Toledo, Ohio. After Mary became a free woman after the Emancipation Proclamation issued by President Abraham Lincoln early in 1863, she went to Toledo to see her childhood friend, who had become Mother Amadeus. The nun found a job for Mary at the Ursuline Catholic convent.

There was a strong bond between Mary and Mother Amadeus, who was fourteen years younger than Black Mary. At the convent, Mary found security, a family, and a sense of belonging. She was already a grown woman, standing six feet tall and weighing about two hundred pounds. She was strong and a good worker, but she had

Mary Fields, sometimes called Black Mary and Stagecoach Mary. She always carried a weapon when delivering the mail. (Courtesy Ursuline Convent Offices, Toledo, Ohio)

learned to cuss and was known to have a short temper. Mary was also a hard drinker. She had learned to be tough, and she knew how to fight. She smoked a pipe and homemade cigars that reportedly smelled awful.

Mother Amadeus and the other sisters apparently tolerated Mary Fields's lifestyle, but in 1884, Mother Amadeus and five other sisters were sent to Montana at the request of Jesuits to establish mission schools on the Cheyenne, Crow, Blackfoot, and Gros Ventre–Assiniboine Reservation in central and eastern Montana.

Near present-day Cascade, Montana, Mother Amadeus became ill with pneumonia while working to establish schools at St. Peter's Mission, which was founded in 1845. Father Damiani at St. Peter's became very concerned about her health and notified the mother superior at the Ursuline convent in Toledo. She came west and brought Mary, who nursed Mother Amadeus back to health.

Mother Amadeus arranged for Mary to work at St. Peter's Mission, freighting supplies, working in the laundry, chopping wood, raising chickens, and doing all sorts of odd jobs. Wherever she went, Mary was armed with at least one pistol. She supposedly received nine dollars a month in wages. One story tells of another hired hand at the mission who received only seven dollars a month. One day in 1894, the hired hand supposedly confronted Mary and asked her why she was worth more money than he was. He also complained to the bishop and made complaints in public about what he thought was an injustice.

One day, Mary saw the dissatisfied hired hand cleaning an outhouse at the mission and decided to shoot him and dump his body into the latrine. She fired and missed. The man fired back, and both emptied their revolvers. Mary was not hit, but the hired man was hit in a buttock when one of her bullets bounced off the mission's stone wall. Other bullets, however, put holes in the bishop's laundry, which hung on a nearby clothesline.

The angry bishop decided it was time for Mary and her short temper to leave. He also did not like her cussing and drinking, nor did he believe she set a good example for the Indian children being schooled at the mission.

The bishop told Mother Amadeus to send Mary away from the mission. She did, but she quietly financed the opening of a café in the town of Cascade. But Mary Fields could not make a profit because she would feed the hungry whether they could pay or not, and the business failed.

Mother Amadeus then asked the government to give Mary Fields the mail route that served the mission. In 1895, she was hired as the U.S. mail coach driver for the Cascade County region, a seventeen-mile route between Cascade and St. Peter's Mission. She reportedly was the first black person hired by the postal service in America to carry the U.S. mail.

For eight years, she drove the mail coach, pulled by her mule, Moses. According to most accounts, she never missed a day on the job. Dressed in a man's hat and coat and carrying a shotgun, she traversed the route in good and bad weather, often smoking a big cigar. Everyone knew her and gave her the nickname "Stagecoach Mary." At age seventy, she retired from the post office.

In 1903, when she was seventy-one, Mary Fields decided to open her own laundry business in Cascade. Tradition has it that everyone in town respected her and paid their bills—all except one man. One day, that man picked up his laundry but failed to pay. Later in the day, she found the man drinking in a local saloon. Cascade saloons were for men only, but the mayor of Cascade had given Mary Fields permission to patronize saloons in the town. When she saw the customer who failed to pay his bill standing at the bar, she walked over to him and knocked him flat with one punch. She then told everyone in the bar his laundry bill was paid.

In 1912, her laundry burned down, but neighbors and friends rebuilt it for her. About that time, she became friends with a young boy whose father owned a ranch outside of Helena. The boy had been born in Helena in 1901 and later became the well-known Hollywood actor Gary Cooper. He spoke and wrote fondly of Stagecoach Mary later in his life after she had died.

Mary Fields's death came on December 5, 1914, in Cascade. She was buried in Hillside Cemetery, located on a hill above St. Peter's Mission, where she had gained the reputation of being a strong woman who beat the odds on the frontier.

37

Ogallala, a Nebraska Cattle Town

The Kansas towns of Abilene, Ellsworth, Newton, Wichita, and Dodge City are well-known cattle towns of the nineteenth century. In southwest Nebraska, however, there was another cattle town that lasted longer than any of those in Kansas. It is Ogallala, and it got its name from the Ogala Sioux Indian tribe. The Indians spelled the name "Ogala" but pronounced it "Oklada."

Although at least two other Nebraska towns along the Union Pacific railroad—Schuyler and Kearney—became shipping points for Texas cattle driven north, the drovers created problems for the settlers who moved into the areas around both towns. To resolve the problems, the Nebraska legislature passed its first herd law in 1872, which required cattlemen to restrain their animals from trespassing on cultivated land. Texas drovers began looking for someplace farther west where there were no homesteaders.

In those years, the hundredth meridian pretty much marked the western north-south boundary for homesteading. East of that line, the land was viewed as arable, but west of the hundredth meridian, the land was semiarid and generally avoided by homesteaders. One hundred miles west of the hundredth meridian was a stop on the Union Pacific transcontinental railroad. Only a railroad section house and a water tank marked the place that became Ogallala.

In the spring of 1868, the Lonergan brothers and Louis Aufden-garten arrived at Ogallala. The first herd of Texas longhorns was brought to Ogallala by Tom and Phillip Lonergan, who wintered their herd west of the Ogallala railroad stop in 1870. They found that the animals survived on the winter brown grasses, which were rich in nourishment. The following year, Tom Lonergan was appointed the Union Pacific railroad agent in Ogallala. Meanwhile, Louis Aufden-garten built a large general store south of the railroad tracks in Ogallala to cater to buffalo hunters.

After the Nebraska legislature passed the herd law in 1872, Ogallala seemed to be everyone's pick for a cattle town. The Union Pacific built cattle pens and loading chutes just west of town, and Phillip Lonergan was hired to run them. The Lonergans also opened a drovers' supply store. By then, Ogallala had become important because south from town ran the major trail to the Platte River.

By 1873, the small population of Ogallala—about twenty-five people—petitioned the governor to create Keith County around Ogallala so they could establish local government and define land ownership. The county was named for M. C. Keith, a local rancher. The county was organized, an election held, and a board of commissioners selected.

An English journalist, Edwin A. Curley, who crossed Nebraska in 1873, arrived in Ogallala on December 9 of that year and later wrote that the town had consisted of a half-dozen buildings, including two eating establishments, but no hotel. One of the eating establishments was located in the railroad station, where meals were also provided for passengers on the railroad's dinner stop for westbound trains.

The Lonergan brothers invited Curley to spend the night in their store, where he could sleep in the attic or loft. Several other travelers also spent the night in the store. Curley later noted that the stove on the main floor kept the downstairs warm, but he and others sleeping in the loft needed several blankets.

By late 1873, the Union Pacific was advertising its cattle pens at Ogallala, but it was not until June 1875 that herds of Texas longhorns began arriving. That year, seventy-five thousand cattle were handled by the railroad yards in Ogallala.

After some local residents offered a free lot to anyone willing to build a business in Ogallala, S. S. Gast of North Platte, Nebraska, obtained a lot and built a large hotel and dining room. He called his hotel the Ogallala House. His wife, a fine cook, made the dining room a popular place for meals.

South of the railroad tracks, Ogallala took shape. Other businesses soon were built in 1875, including the Cowboy's Rest and Crystal Palace saloons. Another new building was the county jail, which was built of stone and had a boilerplate door. The locals believed it was the strongest jail west of Omaha. A man named George Carothers became sheriff in the summer of 1875, but the growing seasonal cattle trade made law enforcement difficult. In fact, during 1875, the county had five sheriffs.

Being sheriff in Ogallala was not a popular job. One incident reported in the *Nebraskian* published in North Platte told of a cowboy who arrived in Ogallala with a trail herd. The cowboy sought to find another man with whom he had quarreled. When he was found, the cowboy killed the man on the spot with five shots. The cowboy immediately fled Ogallala and headed back to Texas.

According to most accounts, the cowboys who came up the trail were a mixed lot, including Mexicans, Irish, English, black, Cajun, and some Frenchmen from Louisiana. Most seemed to have had a streak of rebelliousness about them, a love of horses and handling cattle, and a distrust of homesteaders. Making their headquarters in one of the town's two saloons, gamblers, drifters, and even outlaws sought to take the cowboys' money. Prostitutes, many posing as dance-hall girls, did the same.

Although a number of sheriffs sought to bring law and order to Ogallala and failed, things did not change until about 1878, when Judge William Gaslin arrived. He had been a lawyer in Maine and came west to homestead in Nebraska in 1871. When his wife refused to endure the hardships of homesteading, she left him. He then devoted his life to law. He was a harsh judge, and his sentences helped to reduce crime. For instance, most horse thieves were given ten years in jail.

Another man who helped to bring law and order to Ogallala was Martin DePriest, who was elected sheriff in 1879. A former

Texas ranger, he was a quiet man with good manners who had been a drover. As a Texan, the drovers and cowboys respected him and pretty much did what he asked of them.

By 1881, Ogallala had six saloons to help quench the thirst of the dusty Texas cowboys when they arrived with their trail herds. In early July 1882, as more than a dozen trail herds were being held in the valley south of Ogallala, bad weather struck in the evening. Heavy rain, lightning, and strong winds ripped through the area. A tornado funnel was sighted on the ground. When the storm passed, the cowboys set out to gather the cattle, only to find that many of the animals had died. When their work was done, the cowboys headed for the saloons in Ogallala. They were exhausted and their tempers short. After a few drinks, things got worse, and quarrels and shootings followed. Sheriff DePriest and his deputy found it difficult to restore order. When the violence ended, two men were dead and several wounded.

In 1883, when the Kansas legislature blocked Texas longhorns from being driven anywhere in the state, Texas herds skirted Kansas and followed a new trail north, just inside the Colorado line to Ogallala. But 1884 pretty much marked the end of Texans driving their longhorns north to Ogallala, especially after a serious epidemic of Texas fever. The epidemic first appeared in Ogallala in July, probably brought by Texas cattle. It spread quickly and caused heavy losses to ranchers in and around Ogallala who had begun putting expensive blooded bulls in their herds. As a cattle town, Ogallala quickly faded, but the memories lived on. The town soon found a new niche as a year-round center of trade for farmers and ranchers in the Platte Valley, a role it still plays today.

38

"California Joe,"
Plainsman and Scout

There were at least two men called "California Joe" in the Old West. One was Truman Head, born about 1820 in Otsego, New York, who later joined the California gold rush and supposedly struck it rich. When the Civil War began, Head took his Sharps rifle and enlisted on the Union side. He joined Colonel Hiram Berdan's sharpshooters but was later discharged because he was too old. He died at San Francisco in 1875.

The other "California Joe," often confused with the first, led a life far more exciting. His real name Moses Embree Milner, he was born in May 1829 at Stanford, Kentucky. From most accounts, Milner headed west in 1843 at about the age of fourteen and in St. Louis joined a party of about a dozen hunters and trappers. He spent the winter learning to hunt, trap, and survive on the plains along the North Platte River. This was about three years after the mountain man era ended because the supply of beaver dwindled. It was also a year when large numbers of emigrants were starting west over the Oregon Trail.

In the spring of 1843, Milner and his party took their pelts to Fort Laramie in modern-day Wyoming to sell them. It was then that Milner joined a larger party of twenty-five trappers led by Jim Baker, a veteran mountain man, heading into the Yellowstone River region.

207

When the group reached the Powder River, they discovered a camp of hostile Blackfeet. Baker, realizing that his group was outnumbered, decided that a surprise attack was best. Leaving two men to watch the packs and supplies, Baker led the others, including Milner, down a small canyon toward the camp.

Baker, Milner, and the rest took the Indians by complete surprise as they charged them. Baker's men then pursued the Indians that fled. When someone spotted an Indian on some high ground in the distance, several trappers fired but missed. Milner, lying down and resting his rifle on a boulder, took a shot. It struck the Indian in the head. Someone estimated the distance at four hundred yards. Needless to say, respect for fifteen-year-old Milner grew that day. Eighteen Indians died, and only one trapper was wounded. The Indian camp was burned.

Later the trappers returned to Fort Laramie, where Milner made his headquarters for the next three years. He and five other trappers then decided to go west to Fort Bridger, located on the Black Fork on the Green River in what is now southwestern Wyoming. The trading post had been built by mountain man James Bridger in 1841, who sold supplies, offered blacksmith repairs to emigrants, and traded with Indians.

Bridger gave Milner a job herding livestock. Each morning, he drove the horses and mules out to a grazing area, checked them several times during the day, and returned them to the corral at Fort Bridger each evening. One day Milner discovered five horses had been stolen. He rushed to inform Bridger, who sounded the alarm. Soon Bridger and twenty of his men, including Milner, caught up with a party of ten renegade Indians with the horses. A running fight lasted some time and six Indians were killed, but the horses were recovered. Milner's animal was shot during the battle, but he killed the Indian who fired the shot. One of Bridger's men was killed and another wounded.

When everyone had returned to the fort, Bridger set out a jug of whiskey to thank his men. The Indians and half-breeds gathered around, begging for drinks. When Milner was given a tin cup of whiskey, a half-breed pushed him over, seized the cup, and gulped the contents. Milner leaped to his feet, drew his revolver, and killed the half-breed. The other half-breeds almost retaliated with their weapons, but Bridger and the others prevented bloodshed.

Early in 1846, Milner left Fort Bridger with a party of trappers bound for Fort Laramie. They were caught in a blizzard. Three of the trappers and all of the packhorses died from the extreme cold, but Milner and eight other men survived and eventually reached Fort Laramie. There Milner found a letter from his family. It informed him that they were moving from Kentucky to Warren County, Missouri, west of St. Louis. Milner joined an outfit bound for St. Louis and left Fort Laramie in April 1846.

When the party reached Fort Leavenworth in early June 1846, they learned that war had been declared against Mexico. Milner forgot about visiting his parents when Doniphan's First Missouri Mounted Volunteers reached Fort Leavenworth some days later. Milner joined the army as a teamster and soon headed west. By late July, Milner had reached Bent's Fort on the Arkansas River, more than five hundred miles west of Fort Leavenworth. The army then peacefully conquered New Mexico and established Fort Marcy on a high spot overlooking Santa Fe.

One day Milner and three other civilians employed by the military left Fort Marcy to go hunting. About noon, they stopped for water at a ranch, only to be fired upon by a Mexican rifleman. It was an apparent trap. When the fighting ended, several Mexicans were dead. Milner and the other men rounded up twenty-five horses and headed back to Santa Fe and Fort Marcy, where they were cheered by American troops.

When Colonel Alexander Doniphan heard of their exploits, he called them in and congratulated them. Doniphan, impressed with young Milner, appointed him as a guide. Milner went with Doniphan's expedition as it invaded Mexico and later returned to the United States. It was then that Milner went to St. Louis and on to Warren County in search of his parents. He found them, and there was a joyful reunion. Milner remained with his parents during late 1847 and early 1848.

In the spring of 1848, Milner said good-bye to his parents and returned to St. Louis. There he joined up with a party of men setting out to trap along the North Platte River. On Brady Island, located in the Platte River about twenty-three miles east of modern North Platte, Nebraska, they built a cabin. Tradition says the island was named for a trapper named Brady who had been murdered there by a French companion during a quarrel in the early 1830s.

With the cabin as headquarters, Milner traded with Indians along the Platte and Republican Rivers, as well as other streams in the region. Milner and the other men reportedly fought Sioux Indians and even hunted buffalo, impressing the Indians with how their rifles could kill so many of the shaggies in a short period of time.

By the fall of 1848, Milner was heading back to St. Louis to sell pelts and visit his parents again. He reached their home in time for Christmas. He intended to stay only until spring. Milner, however, met Nancy Emma Watts, who was nearly fourteen. She lived with her parents on a farm adjoining the Milner place. The following spring, on his twenty-fifth birthday, May 8, 1850, they were married, and the next day, they set out for the goldfields of California.

Although some writers have embellished Milner and his wife's journey to California as dangerous because of Indian raids, the trip was mostly uneventful. They arrived safely, and Milner left his wife in Sacramento while he went to the goldfields. Milner found considerable gold and quit prospecting in 1852. He took his wife to Oregon, where they acquired two hundred twenty acres of land, built a cabin, and established a cattle ranch near Corvallis. It was there in October 1853 that his wife gave birth to the first of four sons. By the time the fourth son was born in 1859 at Corvallis, Milner owned a livery stable there and operated a pack train business going to and from mining camps near Walla Walla and into the nearby mountains.

Milner frequently left his wife and family to satisfy his wanderlust. When gold strikes occurred on the Salmon River and around Bannack in modern Montana, he followed. It was near Bannack that he fought three claim jumpers, killing one and wounding another. It was at Virginia City, Montana, that Milner gained the nickname "California Joe" after refusing to give some men his real name. He thought they were seeking revenge for the dead claim jumpers. He liked the nickname and kept his real name and background to himself. When he killed another man for kicking a dog in Virginia City in 1862, vigilantes ran Milner out of town.

California Joe returned to Oregon frequently to see his wife and family and to look after business matters, but he never stayed long. He wandered across much of the West. On November 26, 1864, California Joe was with Kit Carson in the first battle of Adobe Walls on the South Canadian River in modern Hutchinson County, Texas. By the late 1860s, he was working as a scout for the U.S. Army in Kansas. During this time he apparently met and became friends with William F. "Buffalo Bill" Cody.

Cody's sister, Helen Cody Wetmore, wrote in her book *Last of the Great Scouts: The Life of Col. William F. Cody* (1899) that California Joe was a man "of wonderful physique, straight and stout as a pine. His red-brown hair hung in curls below his shoulders; he wore a full beard, and his keen sparkling eyes were of the brightest hue. He came from an Eastern family, and possessed a good education, somewhat rusty from disuse."

About 1867, California Joe met James B. "Wild Bill" Hickok for the first time, probably at Fort Riley, Kansas. The two men became friends and later were seen together on several occasions at Fort Hays and in nearby Hays City, Kansas.

When California Joe first met Lieutenant Colonel George Custer at Fort Hays in 1868, Custer took a liking to Joe and wrote about him in his book *Life on the Plains* (1874):

> There was one among their number whose appearance would have attracted the notice of any casual observer. He was a man about forty years of age, perhaps older, over six feet in height, and possessing a well-proportioned frame. His head was covered with a luxuriant crop of long, almost black hair, strongly inclined to curl, and so long as to fall carelessly over his shoulders. His face, at least so much of it as was not concealed by the long, waving brown beard and mustache, was full of intelligence and pleasant to look upon. His eye was undoubtedly handsome, black and lustrous, with an expression of kindness and mildness combined. On his head was generally to be seen, whether awake or asleep, a huge sombrero, or black slouch hat. A soldier's overcoat, with its large circular cape, a pair of trousers with the legs tucked in the top of his long boots, usually constituted the make-up of the man whom I selected as chief scout. He was known by the euphonious title of "California Joe," no other name seemed ever to have been given him, and no other name appeared to be necessary.

It is interesting that Cody describes Joe's hair as red whereas Custer said it was black. All other descriptions located indicate Milner's hair was red.

In 1868, before the Washita campaign, Custer appointed California Joe chief of scouts. But within hours, he heard that Joe was drunk and demoted him. California Joe missed the Battle of the Washita.

The following year, 1869, California Joe guided General Phillip H. Sheridan from Camp (later Fort) Sill east to Fort Arbuckle for a quick inspection. Fort Arbuckle, in central Indian Territory, was going to be closed in favor of a new post that is today Fort Sill in southwestern Oklahoma. Sheridan wrote in his *Memoirs*,

> I was ready to return immediately to Camp Sill. But my departure was delayed by California Joe, who, notwithstanding the prohibitory laws of the Territory, in some unaccountable way had got gloriously tipsy, which caused a loss of time that disgusted me greatly; but as we could not well do without Joe, I put off starting till the next day, by which time it was thought he would sober up. But I might just as well have gone at first, for at the end of twenty-four hours the incorrigible old rascal was still dead drunk.
>
> How he had managed to get the grog to keep up his spree was a mystery which we could not solve, though we had had him closely watched, so I cut the matter short by packing him into my ambulance and carrying him off to Camp Sill.

In spite of his drinking problem, Sheridan liked California Joe and described him as "an invaluable guide and Indian fighter whenever the clause of the statute prohibiting liquors in the Indian country happened to be in full force."

California Joe remained friends with Sheridan and Custer. In fact, California Joe exchanged several letters with Custer before the Battle of the Little Bighorn. Milner's poor spelling was a source of amusement to Custer.

In the spring of 1870, California Joe went to Colorado, where he and a man named George Wilson prospected for gold. About two years later, they learned of a new strike in Nevada that created a new boomtown called Pioche. They headed there. At Salt Lake City, Milner and Wilson bought twelve hundred cattle, hired some cowboys, and drove the cattle to near Pioche. They established a ranch from which to supply cattle to the hungry miners.

In June 1873, Milner's wife and their second son traveled from Oregon to Nevada and found California Joe waiting for them. His wife and son witnessed a shooting match won by California Joe. He received the purse and the title "Best All-Around Shot in the West." When his wife and son left for California, he promised he would see them in the fall. He then sold his share of the cattle to his partner, George Wilson, and started for California, only to be sidetracked by an offer to guide a prospecting party into New Mexico. When he completed his guiding responsibilities, California Joe went to San Francisco to see his wife and son before they returned to Oregon. He then left to follow a new gold strike in the mountains of California. He apparently had little success and went to Wyoming, where he engaged in wagon freighting until a partner tried to rob him.

When California Joe heard that gold had been discovered in the Black Hills of what is now South Dakota, he and three other men headed there. They reached the site of modern Crook City, only to be attacked by Sioux Indians. One of the men was killed, but Milner and the remaining two fled to Fort Laramie. There, in the spring of 1875, Milner was hired to guide Professor Walter P. Jenney's Black Hills expedition, which had been authorized by the Bureau of Indian Affairs to determine the extent and value of the gold deposits there.

The New York *Herald* printed a story in 1875 from its correspondent, R. B. Davenport, who accompanied the Newton-Jenney expedition to the Black Hills. Davenport reported on an animal skeleton that Milner had given him. Milner, with a straight face, identified the skeleton, which in truth was that of a bull elk, as belonging to a "camelce," a cross between an American elk and a camel once used with others as pack animals in the deserts of Arizona. Davenport bought the story hook, line, and sinker, wrote an article about the find, and sent it off to his New York newspapers, where it was published. Milner enjoyed a good laugh. Davenport did not.

Dr. Valentine T. McGillycuddy, an army surgeon acquainted with California Joe, remembered that the scout had "an intuitive knowledge of country, over regions he had never visited." He also remembered he was "brave, self-reliant, and faithful. His skill as a scout, trailer [tracker], and marksman is attested by all under whom

"California Joe" as he appeared in the spring of 1875 when he was hired to guide Professor Walter P. Jenney's Black Hills expedition. The goal of the government expedition was to determine the extent and value of gold deposits in the Black Hills. (Courtesy Western History Collections, University of Oklahoma Libraries)

he served." Joe was not an easy man to miss: he stood more than six feet in height, was slouchy of dress, and was ever smoking a pipe—often while chewing tobacco at the same time. He usually rode a mule and said little of his past.

When California Joe learned that Custer and his command died in the Battle of the Little Bighorn on June 25, 1876, he supposedly said, "If I had waited at Fort Lincoln for Custer to return and gone with him as his chief scout, I don't think such a thing would have happened."

A few weeks after the Custer battle, California Joe was in Deadwood, where he saw his old friend, Wild Bill Hickok. They talked about the death of Custer. California Joe then told Hickok he was going to Crook City and invited him to go along. Hickok declined. While California Joe was away, Hickok was shot and killed by Jack McCall while playing cards in a Deadwood saloon. A week before he was killed, Hickok was heard to remark to a friend, "I have two trusty friends; one is my six-shooter and the other California Joe."

When California Joe returned to Deadwood, he learned the details, including the fact that Jack McCall had been found not guilty of

Moses Embree Milner, otherwise known as "California Joe," in 1876. This photograph was taken in Bismarck, Dakota Territory, a few months before he was shot dead by Tom Newcomb. (Courtesy Western History Collections, University of Oklahoma Libraries)

killing Hickok, perhaps because Deadwood was located on Indian land. The jury may have thought the trial was illegal. Regardless, Mc-Call was later arrested and tried at Yankton, Dakota Territory, found guilty, and hanged in March 1877. The Cheyenne *Daily Leader,* August 26, 1876, reported:

> Could California Joe have arrived in time, no doubt McCall would have been hanged. . . . After hearing all the particulars of the killing of Wild Bill, [Joe] walked down to McCall's cabin, and calling him out asked him if he didn't think the air about there was rather light for him. McCall's cheeks blanched, and he feebly answered he thought it was. "Well, I guess you have better take a walk then," said Joe, and seating himself on the side of the hill he watched the retreating figure out of sight.

By early fall, California Joe was at Camp (later Fort) Robinson, Nebraska. There he met an old enemy, Tom Newcomb, the post's butcher, who had once falsely accused him of murdering a Frenchman who had married an Indian woman. Dr. McGillycuddy was there and later recalled that the feud broke out again at the bar of the Post Trader on October 29, 1876.

Newcomb threatened to shoot the scout, but California Joe called out, "Drop your gun, Tom, line up here and take a drink." Newcomb did, and the crisis passed. However, about an hour later, Dr. McGillycuddy heard a shot near the corral. He rushed to the scene of the shots and found California Joe on his face, dead, shot in the back. Newcomb was arrested but later released.

When Dr. McGillycuddy removed California Joe's clothes preparatory to an autopsy, he found papers proving that the scout's real name was Moses Embree Milner. California Joe was buried in the post cemetery, and a red cedar headboard marked his grave. Years later, Milner's remains were moved to the Fort McPherson National Cemetery east of North Platte, Nebraska. Today the grave is marked by a stone with the name Moses Milner, without any reference to him being California Joe.

39

The Badlands Rancher Who Became President

The sun had not yet come up on the morning of September 7, 1883, when a twenty-five-year-old New Yorker got off the Northern Pacific train at the frontier town of Little Missouri, located on the west bank of the Little Missouri River in what is now western North Dakota. The young man was Theodore Roosevelt, who had graduated from Harvard three years earlier. He had come west to hunt buffalo.

Young Roosevelt found a room in the Pyramid Park Hotel, freshened up, and then slept a few hours before looking over the town that had sprung up about a year earlier, just before a small nearby military post was abandoned. The small post, known as the Badlands Cantonment, with about fifty soldiers, had been established late in 1879 to protect railroad construction workers. Roosevelt inspected the newer settlement of Medora on the east bank of Little Missouri River, where new buildings were being constructed. He found an air of business and excitement in Medora, but he found no town government and no law and order. Cattle and horse rustling and theft were rampant because the criminal class outnumbered those in town who wanted law and order. Roosevelt's reaction to these conditions is not known, but the next day, he hired Joe Ferris as a guide and rode south of Little Missouri to hunt buffalo in the Badlands.

For more than a week, Roosevelt, Joe Ferris, and his brother, Sylvane, along with William Merrifield rode in search of buffalo among the buttes, mesas, and washes, and through the sharply eroded valleys that had been carved for centuries by the Little Missouri River and its tributaries. It rained every day. Roosevelt chased one old buffalo bull but missed hitting the animal when he fired his weapon at it while riding over rough terrain. Then too, Roosevelt's eyesight was not that good. Three days later, Roosevelt spotted another large bull and killed the shaggy.

The young and unknown New Yorker spent nights in the ranch house of Gregor Lang, who had arrived months earlier from Scotland to manage a ranch for Sir John Pender. Roosevelt and Lang talked much about prospects for cattle raising in the Badlands. Before his hunt ended, Roosevelt decided to become a cattle raiser. He wanted to hire Lang and his son Lincoln to manage his cattle, but they were already committed to taking care of Sir John Pender's cattle.

At Lang's suggestion, Roosevelt entered into an agreement with William Merrifield and Sylvane Ferris, who operated the Maltese Cross Ranch southwest of Medora, after buying out the interests of two other men who owned the ranch. Roosevelt, however, did not get title to much land in the deal. Aside from the ranch house, the Maltese Cross Ranch had open rangeland owned by the government and the railroad. Roosevelt invested about $12,000 to buy four hundred cattle for the ranch. Merrifield and Ferris agreed to care for the cattle for seven years, after which four hundred cattle, or their equivalent in value, were to be returned to Roosevelt. Merrifield and Ferris would then receive half increase in the herd.

Invigorated by his western trip and pleased with his new endeavor, Roosevelt returned to the East, where he was elected in November 1883 to the New York State Assembly. Early in 1884, however, he suffered a personal tragedy. On a February night, both Roosevelt's mother and his wife died. He was devastated, and during the weeks that followed, he thought of the West as an escape from his sorrows. He decided that if his cattle wintered well in the Little Missouri River Badlands, he would start another ranch in the region.

After attending the Republican National Convention in Chicago as a delegate, Roosevelt took a train west to Medora in June 1884. Medora and Little Missouri had grown during the eight months

Roosevelt had been in the East. Both towns now had eighty-four buildings, including three hotels. Medora, the largest, had more than two hundred residents. Much of the growth was due to the creation of a packing plant and other businesses established by the Marquis de Mores, a Frenchman who founded Medora in 1883; he named the town after his wife, Medora von Hoffman, the daughter of a wealthy New York banker. Mores and Medora had married in 1882, a year before he traveled west to the Badlands of Dakota Territory, where he purchased land at the junction of the Little Missouri River and the Northern Pacific railroad to establish the town of Medora. There he built a packinghouse and organized the Northern Pacific Refrigerator Car Company. Mores began shipping dressed meat east by refrigerator car after establishing a chain of ice houses and cold-storage buildings along the Northern Pacific line east of Medora.

Although some writers have characterized Roosevelt's relationship with the Marquis de Mores as unfriendly, aside from an exchange of letters of September 1885 in which Roosevelt assured Mores he was not his enemy, the available evidence suggests their relationship was amicable. Roosevelt is known to have visited Mores and his wife at their home, the Chateau de Mores, across the Little Missouri River west of Medora.

On his second trip to Medora in June 1884, Roosevelt went to his Maltese Cross Ranch, located southwest of Medora, to plan an expansion of his ranching operations. In a letter to his sister, Anna Cowles, Roosevelt related that he had lost about twenty-five head of cattle from wolves and cold weather the previous winter, but the rest of his cattle had done well. He wrote that he planned to buy "a thousand more cattle" and make ranching his regular business.

Roosevelt soon established a second ranch, which he named Elkhorn, on government land about twenty-five miles north of Medora. By late summer, he sent Ferris and Merrifield, his ranch foremen, to Iowa to purchase a thousand head of cattle. Meanwhile, he persuaded two former Maine guides, Wilmot Dow and William Sewall, to become foremen of his Elkhorn Ranch. Within a year, he constructed what was described as the finest ranch house in the Badlands, which he called his Home Ranch House. There he would spend much time when in the Badlands.

Early in 1884, several ranchers in the Badlands thought it was time to establish a stockmen's organization to enforce rules of the open range. The *Bad Lands Cow Boy*, a weekly newspaper established by Arthur Packard, a graduate of the University of Michigan, to serve Little Missouri and Medora, supported the ranchers' efforts. A committee of ranchers decided to draw up bylaws for such an organization, but the matter lagged until Roosevelt returned to the Badlands in 1884. When he learned what had occurred, he called a meeting of the stockmen at Medora on December 19, 1884.

Representatives from eleven cattle ranches attended the meeting and elected Roosevelt chairman of what became known as the Little Missouri River Stockmen's Association. They drew up resolutions and rules for a permanent organization. The minutes of that meeting were written by Roosevelt, and he was given the job of writing the constitution and bylaws. He did so, and after returning to the East, he had the *By-Laws of the Little Missouri River Stockmen's Association* printed in a small six-page booklet by G. P. Putnam's Sons in New York City. Only one copy appears to have survived, and it is in the library at Harvard.

When Roosevelt returned from the East to the Badlands in the spring of 1885, he took part in the cattle roundup on the open range. Because most ranchers were squatters and owned little land, it was necessary to round up all cattle twice a year to separate them according to their brands. The spring roundup in which Roosevelt participated saw the branding of calves and any yearlings that had escaped branding the previous spring, while during the fall roundup, ranchers selected cattle to be driven to market. During the spring roundup in 1885, Roosevelt apparently added more cattle to his herds. The *Bad Lands Cow Boy* reported:

> Fifteen hundred head of steers, yearlings and two's came in Thursday morning for the Elkhorn and Chimney Butte [Maltese Cross] ranches of Theodore Roosevelt. They were in fair condition after their long ride and except for the disadvantage of a large number being yearlings, give every evidence of growing into good beef. The larger majority are steers. A good lot of Short-horn bulls and one Polled-Angus were in the herd. A thousand of these cattle will be driven to the Elkhorn ranch and five hundred to the already well-stocked Chimney Butte [Maltese Cross] ranch.

During 1885, Roosevelt was reelected chair of the Little Missouri Stockmen's Association, but he spent the winter of 1885 and

Theodore Roosevelt as a cattle rancher in what is now North Dakota. This photograph was taken while Roosevelt was on a cattle roundup. (Courtesy Theodore Roosevelt Collection, Harvard College Library)

1886 in New York City. When he returned to the Badlands in March 1886, he found that cattle losses had been light during what had been a rather mild winter, which pleased him. His cattle ranching appears to have reached its peak by early 1886. For a total investment of about $82,500, Roosevelt and his foremen owned between three thousand and five thousand cattle—better than average for cattle ranchers in the region.

The year 1886 saw Roosevelt elected president of the Little Missouri Stockmen's Association, and he again participated in the spring roundup, this time serving as cocaptain. On June 7, 1886, in a letter to his sister, Roosevelt wrote:

> I have been on the roundup for a fortnight and really enjoy the work greatly; in fact I am passing a most pleasant summer, though I miss all of you very, very much. We breakfast at three every

morning, and work from sixteen to eighteen hours a day, count-
ing night guard; so I get pretty sleepy; but I feel strong as a bear.

It was during the summer of 1886 that Roosevelt and his foremen, Sewall and Dow, caught three men who had stolen a boat from
the Elkhorn Ranch. Unable to take the prisoners to the sheriff at
Dickinson because of ice jams on the Little Missouri River, Roosevelt
and his foremen remained in camp until they obtained a wagon from
the Diamond C Ranch. The three men were then turned over to the
sheriff at Dickinson. The men were later tried in Mandan, and two
were sent to prison.

During July 1886, the *Dickinson Press* and a few other newspapers
in Dakota Territory reported favorably on a speech Roosevelt made
during the Fourth of July celebration at Dickinson. That summer at
the Maltese Cross Ranch, he also finished writing his book, *Hunting
Trips of a Ranchman,* printed in an edition of five hundred copies in
1885 and reprinted in 1886 and later. He also wrote several articles
for *Century* and *Outlook* magazines while at the ranch.

Roosevelt returned to New York City late in the summer of 1886
to receive the Republican nomination for mayor of New York City.
When the election was held in November, he lost. The following
month, he married Edith Carow in England and went to Europe for
a long winter honeymoon, but it was there he received reports that
most of his cattle had died during a hard winter on the northern
plains. Roosevelt returned to the United States and went straight to
Medora. From there he wrote his friend Henry Cabot Lodge, "Well,
we have had a perfect smashup all through the cattle country of the
northwest. The losses are crippling. For the first time I have been utterly
unable to enjoy a visit to my ranch. I shall be glad to get home."

Members of the Little Missouri Stockmen's Association agreed
not to hold a general spring roundup because they believed most of
their cattle had drifted with the storm. Ranchers who searched for
their cattle during the summer found only carcasses. Later, one esti-
mate by the *Mandan Pioneer* reported that perhaps 75 percent of the
cattle on the northern plains had been lost. It had been a bad winter
for cattlemen not only in North Dakota, but elsewhere on the plains.

Roosevelt's losses were so great that he decided to get out of
cattle ranching. At some point between 1890 and 1892, Roosevelt

abandoned the Elkhorn Ranch and shifted his activities to the Maltese Cross Ranch. In an effort to recoup his losses, Roosevelt, together with R. H. M. Ferguson, Archibald D. Russell, and Douglas Robinson, organized the Elkhorn Ranch Company, which was incorporated under the laws of New York. Roosevelt transferred his cattle holdings, valued at $16,500, to the company, and he later invested an additional $10,200. The company's manager was Sylvane Ferris.

Although Roosevelt made visits to the Badlands in 1892, 1893, and 1896, his political activities in the East made it difficult for him to travel west and to give attention to his ranching interests. When President William McKinley appointed him assistant secretary of the navy in 1897, Roosevelt decided to sell out his ranching interests. He wrote Sylvane Ferris, suggesting he dispose of all the cattle on the ranch during 1898. Early in that year, when the United States went to war with Spain and Roosevelt made a name for himself with his Rough Riders in Cuba, he sold his cattle interest to Sylvane Ferris. In all, Roosevelt had invested more than $82,000 in his ranches and lost about $50,000.

Before the nineteenth century ended, the government began surveying much of the Little Missouri Badlands. The Northern Pacific railway began selling its lands in the area as the region was opened to homesteaders. The days of the open range in the Little Missouri Badlands ended and most of the large cattle ranches went out of business. Meanwhile, in the East, Roosevelt's fame with the Rough Riders in Cuba saw him nominated as the vice presidential running mate with President William McKinley, who won. Roosevelt's life changed dramatically on September 6, 1901, when McKinley was shot by an assassin in Buffalo, New York. Eight days later, when McKinley died, forty-two-year-old Roosevelt became the twenty-sixth president of the United States and is today remembered as one of the strongest and most vigorous presidents in the nation's history. The Little Missouri Badlands rancher had come a long way.

NOTES

1. Jim Fugate's Adventures on the Santa Fe Trail

James M. Fugate's recollections are contained in Bernard Bryan Smyth's 168-page book *The Heart of the New Kansas: A Pamphlet Historical and Descriptive of Southwestern Kansas* (Great Bend, Kans.: B. B. Smyth, 1880). In 1880, Fugate was living in Barton County, Kansas.

2. How the Staked Plains Got Their Name

Material on Coronado came from Herbert E. Bolton, *Coronado on the Turquoise Trail: Knight of Pueblos and Plains* (Albuquerque: University of New Mexico Press, 1949); and W. C. Holden, "Coronado's Route across the Staked Plains," *Bulletin of West Texas Historical Association* 20 (October 1944). Also helpful was John Miller Morris, *El Llano Estacado: Exploration and Imagination on the High Plains of Texas and New Mexico, 1536–1860* (Austin: Texas State Historical Association, 1997); and Walter Prescott Webb, ed., *The Handbook of Texas* (Austin: Texas State Historical Association, 1952–76), 3 vols. Other sources are cited in the story.

3. The Ride of "Portugee" John Phillips

A lengthy study of Phillips can be found in Robert A. Murray, "The John 'Portuguese' Phillips Legends," *Annals of Wyoming* 40 (April 1968). See also a more recent examination of Phillips: John D. McDermott, *Civilian, Military, Native American Portraits of Fort Phil Kearny* (Banner, Wyo.: Bozeman Trail Association, 1993), 88–92. Newspaper clippings in my files provided additional information, along with records relating to the government's settlement of Phillips's claim against Indian depredations at his Wyoming ranch. Phillips's widow, Hattie, eventually moved to Los Angeles, California, where she died in 1936 at the age of ninety-four. A story of her death appears in the *Wyoming Tribune,* January 17, 1936.

4. The Texan Who Invaded New Mexico

Webb, ed., *Handbook of Texas*, provides a brief biography of John Hittson, but many other sources contain information on his invasion of New Mexico, including Charles Kenner, "The Great New Mexico Cattle Raid, 1872," *New Mexico Historical Review* 37 (October 1962); and his "John Hittson: Cattle King of West Texas," *West Texas Historical Association Year Book* 37 (1961). Joseph G. McCoy makes reference to Hittson in his classic book *Historic Sketches of the Cattle Trade of the West and Southwest* (Kansas City, Mo.: Ramsey, Millett, and Hudson, 1874). M. L. Johnson provides some interesting recollections as a cowboy for Hittson in *Trail Blazing: A True Story of the Struggles with Hostile Indians on the Frontier of Texas* (Dallas: Mathis Publishing Company, 1935).

5. How Cowboys Came to Sing

Many sources were consulted, including Austin E. and Alta S. Fife, *Ballads of the Great West* (Palo Alto, Calif.: American West Publishing Co., 1970), and their *Cowboy and Western Songs: A Comprehensive Anthology* (New York: Bramhall House, 1982); Alan Lomax, *The Folk Songs of North America* (New York: Doubleday, 1960), and two books by his father, John A. Lomax, *Songs of the Cattle Trail and Cow Camp* (New York: Macmillan, 1919) and *Cowboy Songs and Other Frontier Ballads* (New York: Macmillan, 1930); Guy Logsdon, *"The Whorehouse Bells Were Ringing" and Other Songs Cowboys Sing* (Urbana: University of Illinois Press, 1989); Glenn Ohrlin, *The Hell-Bound Train: A Cowboy Songbook* (Urbana: University of Illinois Press, 1973); Jim Bob Tinsley, *He Was Singin' This Song* (Orlando: University Presses of Florida, 1981); and W. Howard "Jack" Thorp, *Songs of the Cowboys, Variants, Commentary, Notes and Lexicon by Austin E. and Alta S. Fife* (New York: Clarkson N. Potter, Inc., 1966). This book contains a copy of the first printed collection of cowboy songs, published by Thorp in 1908. Material on Frank Maynard can be found in James Hoy, "F. H. Maynard, Author of 'The Cowboy's Lament,'" *Mid-America Folklore* 21, no. 2 (fall 1993): 61–68.

6. A Trail Drive Honeymoon

Scattered articles have been written about D. W. "Doc" Barton's life, but no full-blown biography has been attempted, perhaps because facts are scattered and details of his life are difficult to locate. One of the earliest articles on Barton was "A Cattle Drive from Texas to Kansas," *Kansas City Star*, November 14, 1926. An unidentified staff correspondent interviewed Barton and his wife in their small cottage at the southeast corner of Ingalls, Kansas, and a photographer took the couple's photograph. The writer of the article, however, identified Barton as "D.M.," not "D.W." Later, Charles C. Isely, a Kansas journalist, interviewed Barton for an undated article entitled "'Doc' Barton, the Last of the Cattle Kings," found in the clippings file of the Kansas State Historical Society, Topeka. William E. Connelley, *A Standard History of Kansas and Kansans* (Chicago: Lewis Publishing, 1919), rev. ed., 5:25–30, contains a brief biography of Barton. However, it contains some incorrect information, as does Ida Rath, *Early Ford County* (Dodge City, Kans.: Ford County Historical Society,

1964). Additional information on the Bartons can be found in Leola Howard Blanchard, *Conquest of Southwest Kansas: A History and Thrilling Stories of Frontier Life in the State of Kansas* (Wichita, Kans.: Wichita Eagle Press, 1931). Webb, ed., *Handbook of Texas*, also contains biographies of D. W. Barton and Alfred H. Barton, with much information on their lives in Texas. Some additional information was found in Harry E. Chrisman, *Lost Trails of the Cimarron* (Denver: Sage Books, 1961).

7. When Billy Carried the News

This story was apparently printed for the first time under the headline "A Perilous Ride" in the *St. Joseph Gazette*, January 24, 1897. It was later reprinted in *Gray's Doniphan County History*, compiled by P. L. Gray (Bendena, Kans.: Roycroft Press, 1905). Efforts to identity our "Billy" have not been successful.

8. When Women Were Scarce

Most of the sources are mentioned in the story. Jack Potter's recollections came from his *Trails of the Old West* (Clayton, N.M.: Leader Press, 1939).

9. The Tres Piedras Legend

The family Bible of José Lopat appears to be the source of the Tres Piedras legend. Tres Piedras, or "Three Stones," refers to the three stone markers, each containing about fifteen large rocks and stretching over a distance of perhaps one-quarter of a mile. In about 1962, a fourth marker was found. Perhaps the earliest written version of the story was published as "The Tres Piedras Legend," *Oklahoman* (Oklahoma City, Oklahoma Territory), September 27, 1903, approximately four years before Oklahoma became a state. A more comprehensive and up-to-date account was later compiled by Steve Wilson, *Oklahoma Treasures and Treasure Tales* (Norman: University of Oklahoma Press, 1976).

10. Treasure Tales from the Dakotas

Sources for these tales came from the publications of the North and South Dakota historical societies, undated newspaper clippings, and treasure tales told by the late Jesse Ed Rascoe and printed by the late Ed Bartholomew in Texas.

11. The Virginia Dale Legend

A good deal of information on the Virginia Dale stage station came from the Colorado Historical Society and from J. V. Frederick, *Ben Holladay, the Stagecoach King, a Chapter in the Development of Transcontinental Transportation* (Glendale, Calif.: Arthur H. Clark Co., 1940). Other information came from two works about Jack Slade: Robert Scott, *Slade! The True Story of the Notorious Badman* (Glendo, Wyo.: High Plains Press, 2004); and an earlier biography by Kenneth Jessen and Roy Paul O'Dell, *An Ear in*

His Pocket: The Life of Jack Slade (Loveland, Colo.: JV Publications, 1996). Mark Twain's references to Slade were found in *Roughing It* (Hartford, Conn.: American Publishing, 1872).

12. Did Henry Starr Leave a Buried Treasure?

Starr's own book *Thrilling Events; Life of Henry Starr . . .* (Tulsa, 1914, privately printed), a 50-page work, is a well-written and interesting look at the author during his early years. He ends his narrative with a bitter attack against society, with many negative comments about graft in the courts, especially that of Judge Parker in Fort Smith. It provided source material for this story, along with early newspaper articles from the *Tulsa World*, the *Daily Oklahoman*, and the *Kansas City Star*. Also helpful was Glenn Shirley, *Henry Starr: Last of the Real Badmen* (New York: David McKay Co., 1965).

13. The Stage Station Treasure

Much of this tale was found in two undated newspaper clippings from the 1930s plus material found in the files of the Kansas State Historical Society and in my book, *The Santa Fe Trail: Its History, Legends, and Lore* (New York: Alfred A. Knopf, 2000).

14. The Sheepherder's Treasure

This tale is tucked away in Robert G. Ferguson, *Lost Treasures: The Search for Hidden Gold*. The author paid Vantage Press to publish the book in 1957 when he was eighty-two years old and living in Iveson, Arizona. He died there four years later.

15. Legend of "The Cave"

Larry Potter, *History of Hope, Kansas* (Hope, Kans.: Privately printed, 1997), provided the basic information for this legend. Additional information came from an interview with Mr. Potter on May 20, 2006. A review of the *Kansas Historical Collections* and *Kansas Quarterly* failed to turn up any account of gold seekers returning east from California after having been attacked in Dickinson County or nearby Marion County, nor has any report of robbers stealing an army payroll in the area been located.

16. The Lost Treasure of the Missouri Traders

I first ran across this story while looking through the *Missouri Republican* in the paper's March 5, 1833, issue. Research turned up references including Josiah Gregg, *Commerce of the Prairies* (1844), 2:49–53, which varies slightly from the earlier newspaper account; and William Waldo, "Recollections," *Glimpses of the Past* (St. Louis: Missouri Historical Society), 5:65–68, which provides some names of those traders in the party. If any of the surviving traders wrote their recollections of their journey, they have not been located.

17. Civilizing No-Man's-Land

Much has been written about No-Man's-Land in what is now the Oklahoma Panhandle. The *Chronicles of Oklahoma* contain much information, including T. E. Beck, "Cimarron Territory" (June 1929), and J. V. Frederick, "The Vigilantes in Early Beaver" (June 1938). Also consulted was Carl Coke Rister, *No Man's Land* (Norman: University of Oklahoma Press, 1948). In addition, the early histories of Oklahoma, including Luther Hill's two-volume *History of the State of Oklahoma* (Chicago, 1908), contained helpful information. My compressed version of the story is not definitive.

18. The Prizefight Texas Didn't Want

The facts of this story were pulled together from various sources, including Albert Bigelow Paine, *Captain Bill McDonald, Texas Ranger* (New York: J. J. Little & Ives, 1909), which includes an appendix with extracts from the official report of the Texas adjutant general on the fight. Walter Prescott Webb, *The Texas Rangers* (New York: Houghton Mifflin Co., 1935), contains additional information, as does the 1958 edition of *The Ring*, a magazine published in New York by Nat Fleischer, and Webb, ed., *Handbook of Texas*. Langtry, Texas, where Judge Roy Bean held court in his saloon, was not named, as Bean supposedly claimed, for the beautiful English singer, Emilie "Lillie" Langtry. The town of Langtry was actually named for George Langtry, an engineer and foreman of the construction crew that built the Southern Pacific line through the area in 1882. Judge Bean did name his saloon the Jersey Lilly in honor of the singer after Bean fell in love with her picture, which he found in a newspaper or magazine.

19. Who Murdered Belle Starr?

My longtime friend, LeRoy Towns, wrote the story of A. J. Robinson's tale for *Midway*, the Topeka *Capital-Journal*, August 2, 1970. At the time, Towns was editor of the Sunday supplement. He later became press secretary to Kansas Governor Robert Bennett and then chief of staff in the Washington office of Kansas U.S. Senator Pat Roberts.

A great deal has been written about Belle Starr. Unfortunately, many accounts are based on a little book entitled *Belle Starr, the Bandit Queen; or, the Female Jesse James* (New York: Richard K. Fox, 1889), and written by an anonymous writer on the *Police Gazette* staff. The book is "historically worthless," according to the late Ramon Adams, a longtime authority on outlaws. Perhaps the most accurate work on Belle Starr is Burton Rascoe, *Belle Starr, "the Bandit Queen"* (New York: Random House, 1941). Another interesting book is William Yancey Shackleford [Randolph Vance], *Belle Starr, the Bandit Queen; the Career of the Most Colorful Outlaw the Indian Territory Ever Knew* (Girard, Kans.: Haldeman-Julius Publications, 1943). Shackleford reviews and compares all material on Belle Starr written before Rascoe's volume was published. He makes no mention of Mrs. Devena and leaves the question of who killed Belle Starr unanswered.

20. Who Was Seth Bullock?

Old-timers in South Dakota know the story of Seth Bullock well, but until the HBO television series *Deadwood* appeared, he was not well known elsewhere. A good source for information is Kenneth C. Kellar, *Seth Bullock: Frontier Marshal* (Aberdeen, S.D.: North Plains Press, 1972). The author is Bullock's grandson, a native of Deadwood. *Theodore Roosevelt, an Autobiography* (New York: Macmillan, 1913), was helpful, as was Kermit Roosevelt, *The Long Trail* (New York, 1921), which includes a chapter on Bullock. Two books about South Dakota also contain material on Bullock, including Estelline Bennett, *Old Deadwood Days* (New York: Charles Scribner, 1935), and George P. Baldwin, ed., *The Black Hills Illustrated* (Chicago: Blakely Publishing Co., 1904). The U.S. marshal's office, District of South Dakota, provided a good biography of Bullock.

21. The Law and Cattle Town Gamblers

Much of the information came from my files on Kansas cattle towns and from Robert Wright, *Dodge City, the Cowboy Capital* (Wichita, Kans., 1913). Some material was taken from my books, *The Buffalo Book True Tales of the Old-Time Plains Cowboy Culture: A Saga of Five Centuries.*

22. When Cowboys Went on Strike

This story is included in my *Buffalo Book.* Webb, ed., *Handbook of Texas,* includes material on the strike, as does B. Byron Price, "Community of Individualists: The Panhandle Stock Association, 1881–1891," in *At Home on the Range,* ed. John R. Wunder (Westport, Conn.: Greenwood Press, 1985).

23. The Cat that Crossed the Plains

This story was told by G. W. Thissell and is tucked away in his privately printed and now rare booklet, *Crossing the Plains in '49* (Oakland, Calif., 1903).

24. Marsh Johnson's First Buffalo Hunt

The primary source for this story is Marsh L. Johnson's 116-page book *Trail Blazing: A True Story of the Struggles with Hostile Indians on the Frontier of Texas* (Dallas: Mathis Publishing Co., 1935). Some of Johnson's recollections were first written in 1918 and were published in a 30-page pamphlet in Dallas in 1923. Later, he put to paper other recollections. With the help of his daughter, Elvia Johnson Pearson, all of Johnson's recollections were published in 1935 in the book cited above. Johnson was born on September 7, 1848, in Comberland County, North Carolina. He was seven years old when he came with his family to Texas in 1855 via ox-drawn wagon.

25. The White Stallion of the Plains

This account by Abraham "Abe" Buford was found in the *New York Times*, June 6, 1882. The story had first appeared in the *Louisville* (Ky.) *Commercial*, reporting on a lecture given by Buford. Captain Nathan Boone does not refer to the story in his official report of August 11, 1843, written at Fort Gibson, but that report does not include unofficial activities by his men. Boone's journal is reprinted in the *Chronicles of Oklahoma* 7, no. 1 (March 1929): 58–105. Buford's obituary was published in the *Louisville Courier-Journal*, June 10, 1884.

26. Wild Buffalo and Other Critters

Many of my sources are included in this story. Josiah Gregg's comments are published in his *Commerce of the Prairies* (2 vols., 1844). Also helpful was James R. Mead, *Hunting and Trading on the Great Plains, 1859–1875*, ed. Schuyler Jones (Norman: University of Oklahoma Press, 1986). I also pulled bits and pieces from my *Buffalo Book*.

27. Tales of Legless Critters

Snake stories are as plentiful as buffalo once were on the plains and prairies of the West. These stories were collected during the last half century and filed away. Some came from pioneer recollections, others from old newspapers, and still others came from the files of several state historical societies or were passed along by friends.

28. The Missing White Buffalo

The story of the Morgans' white buffalo can be found in the *Topeka Capital-Commonwealth*, December 18, 1888. Information on the trophy's later adventures may be found in the *Topeka State Journal*, November 19, 1903. I included the story in my *Buffalo Book*.

29. Grizzly and Black Bear Tales

Some sources are included in the story. The rest came from my collection of bear tales accumulated during the past forty years.

30. The Day Chief Old Wolf Nearly Lost His Scalp

John Hatcher's story about Old Wolf was first put down on paper by Henry Inman in *The Old Santa Fe Trail* (New York, 1897). Other bits and pieces of the story were found in the following: James W. Abert, *Through the Country of the Comanche Indians in the Fall of the Year 1845: The Journal of a U.S. Army Expedition Led by Lieutenant James W. Abert of the Topographical Engineers*, ed. John Galvin (1846; reprint, San Francisco: J. Howell, 1970); Lewis H. Garrard, *Wah-To-Yah and the Taos Trail* (Cincinnati, 1850); and Mildred P. Mayhall, *The Kiowas* (Norman: University of Oklahoma Press, 1962). My first attempt to tell the story about Hatcher and Chief Old Wolf appeared in the Sunday magazine of the *Kansas City Star* in 1974.

31. Two Letters from Abilene

My sources are included in the story.

32. Spotted Tail's Daughter

Appendix A in Eugene Fitch Ware, *The Indian War of 1864* (Topeka: Crane & Co., 1911), contains material by Ware about Ah-Ho-Ap-Pa. Although a native of Connecticut, Ware grew up in Iowa. When the Civil War started, he enlisted in the First Iowa infantry, later served in the Fourth Iowa cavalry, and was mustered out as a captain having served as aide-de-camp to several generals, including Grenville M. Dodge. In his 1911 book, Ware may have embellished his story of Spotted Tail's daughter to add color. I can find no other reference to the daughter being called an Indian "princess." The *Annals of Wyoming* also contains information on Spotted Tail and his daughter, as does the part of the *National Park Service Historical Handbook* relating to Fort Laramie. One account says that in the late 1870s, Spotted Tail retrieved his daughter's bones and took them to the reservation for reburial. In 2000, however, the *Federal Register*, vol. 65, no. 138, reported that the remains of Ah-Ho-Ap-Pa are in the possession of the American Heritage Center at the University of Wyoming, Laramie, and had been donated to the center in 1964 by Elizabeth Oskamp. Her father reportedly collected them years earlier at Fort Laramie.

33. The Nebraska Hoax King

This story is borrowed from my book, *Red Blood and Black Ink: Journalism in the Old West* (New York: Alfred A. Knopf, 1998). A longer account may be found in Louis Pound, "The John G. Maher Hoaxes," *Nebraska History* 33 (1952): 203–19.

34. Fort Mann's Woman Soldier

This story was pieced together from bits and pieces of information found in several sources, including Thomas L. Karnes, "Gilpin's Volunteers on the Santa Fe Trail," *Kansas Historical Quarterly* 30, no. 1 (spring 1964): 5–14; Ann W. Hafen, "John Simpson Smith," in *The Mountain Men and the Fur Trade of the Far West*, ed. LeRoy R. Hafen (Glendale, Calif.: Arthur H. Clark Co., 1968), 5:325–45; First Lieutenant Amandus Schnabel's court-martial record, Bent's Fort, January 4, 1848, in Record Group 94, G368, AGO National Archives; and David Lavender, *Bent's Fort* (Garden City, N.Y.: Doubleday, 1954).

Fort Mann was deserted again in 1848 after Gilpin and his Missouri Volunteers returned east. Less than two years later, Colonel Edwin V. Sumner camped near the decaying ruins of Fort Mann and established Camp Mackay, which was renamed Fort Atkinson in 1851. The post was abandoned two years later after the government signed a treaty with the Indians, but in 1854, the government destroyed the post so Indians would not be able to use it.

35. The Legend of Rawhide

Agnes Wright Spring relates the legend in *The Cheyenne and Black Hills Stage and Express Routes* (Glendale, Calif.: Arthur H. Clark Co., 1949). A slightly different version is related by Virginia Cole Trenholm and Maurine Carley, *Wyoming Pageant* (Casper, Wyo.: Prairie Publishing Co., 1946). A third variation appears in Albert Jerome Dickson, *Covered Wagon Days, a Journey across the Plains in the Sixties, and Pioneer Days in the Northwest*, ed. Arthur Jerome Dickson (Cleveland: Arthur H. Clark Co., 1929). Additional material was provided by the Niobrara County Carnegie Library at Lusk, Wyoming.

36. Black Mary

The story of Mary Fields was pieced together from numerous sources, including material from the public library in Cascade, Montana; the Ursuline Convent Offices in Toledo, Ohio; and the Montana Historical Society. No definitive biography has been written about Mary Fields, but James A. Franks, *Mary Fields: The Story of Black Mary* (Santa Cruz, Calif.: Wild Goose Press, 2000), is a contribution toward that end. Robert H. Miller, *The Story of Stagecoach Mary Fields* (Morristown, N.J.: Silver Press, 1995), tells her story for young people.

37. Ogallala, a Nebraska Cattle Town

Much on Ogallala's history was found in Norbert R. Mahnken, "Ogallala, Nebraska Cowboy Capital," *Nebraska History Quarterly* (April–June 1947). Edwin A. Curley's observations appear in *Nebraska, Its Advantages, Resources, and Drawbacks* (New York: American and Foreign Publication Co., 1875). Additional material was found in Elaine Nielsen's informative history, *Ogallala: A Century on the Trail*, published by the author and the Keith County Historical Society at Ogallala in 1984.

38. "California Joe," Plainsman and Scout

The only biography of Moses Embree "California Joe" Milner is Joe E. Milner and Earle R. Forrest, *California Joe* (Caldwell, Idaho: Caxton, 1935). The University of Nebraska Press reprinted the volume in 1987 with a fine new foreword by Joseph G. Rosa. A compressed biography of Milner appears in Dan L. Thrapp, *Encyclopedia of Frontier Biography* (Glendale, Calif.: Arthur H. Clark Co., 1988), vol. 2. Other bits and pieces came from a variety of works where there is passing mention of California Joe, including Joseph G. Rosa, *They Called Him Wild Bill: The Life and Adventures of James Butler Hickok* (Norman: University of Oklahoma Press, 1974), 2nd rev. ed.; George Armstrong Custer, *My Life on the Plains, or Personal Experiences with Indians* (New York: Sheldon and Co., 1874); General Phillip H. Sheridan, *Personal Memoirs of P. H. Sheridan, General, United States Army* (New York: C. L. Webster & Company, 1888), 2 vols.; Helen Cody Wetmore, *Last of the Great Scouts* (1899); and Joe De Barthe, *Life and Adventures of Frank Grouard* (St. Joseph, Mo., 1894).

Several cheap publications were published during the 1880s about California Joe but are embellished and not factually reliable. They include J. W. Buel, *Heroes of the Plains* (Hartford, Conn.: Historical Publishing Co., 1882); D. M. Kelsey, *Pioneer Heroes* (Hartford, Conn.: Historical Publishing Co., 1882); and Colonel Thomas Hoyer Monstery, *California Joe's First Trail: A Story of the Destroying Angels* (New York: Beadle & Adams, 1884), which is only 15 pages long. In 1885, Beadle & Adams published two other books, Captain Frederick Whittaker, *California Joe* (15 pages), and Colonel Prentis Ingraham, *California Joe, the Mysterious Plainsman: The Strange Adventures of an Unknown Man Whose Real Identity, Like that of the Man in the Iron Mask, Is Still Unsolved* (29 pages). And in 1886, E. G. Cattermole's *Famous Frontiersmen* was published in Chicago and contains some material on California Joe. All of these books were written in the nineteenth-century dime novel style, some for young people, to provide exciting stories about the West. Little attention was paid to factual accuracy.

A lengthy song titled "California Joe" appears in John A. Lomax, *Cowboy Songs* (New York, 1910). The song has since been credited to John W. "Captain Jack" Crawford, *The Poet Scout* (San Francisco, 1879). Crawford claimed the words were based on a story told to him by California Joe about his courtship and marriage.

Hollywood actor Charley Grapwin played the role of California Joe in the 1942 motion picture *They Died with Their Boots On*, which starred Errol Flynn as Custer.

Details are hazy regarding much of Milner's life, including reports of another marriage on July 8, 1848, in Lincoln County, Kentucky, to Emaline Thurman. This would be two years before his marriage on May 8, 1850, to Nancy Emma Watts, who was the mother of Milner's four sons.

39. The Badlands Rancher Who Became President

A slightly different version of this story was written by the author for the late John Jacobs of Brenham, Texas, and was published in 2000 in *By-laws of the Little Missouri River Stockmen's Association*. Many sources were used to piece together this story. They include Chester L. Brooks and Ray H. Mattison, *Theodore Roosevelt and the Dakota Badlands* (Washington, D.C.: National Park Service, 1958); Herman Hagedorn, *Roosevelt in the Badlands* (Boston: Houghton Mifflin Co., 1921); Lincoln Alexander Lang, *Ranching with Roosevelt* (Philadelphia: J. B. Lippincott Company, 1926); Ray H. Mattison, *Roosevelt and the Stockmen's Association,* a separate printing of Mattison's article published in *North Dakota History* 17, nos. 2 and 3 (April–July 1950); Mattison, *Roosevelt's Dakota Ranches*, published by the *Bismarck* (N.D.) *Tribune* in 1957, and his "Ranching in the Dakota Badlands," *North Dakota History* 19, nos. 2 and 3 (April–July 1950). Also of much help were letters written by Theodore Roosevelt, *Cowboys and Kings: Three Great Letters* (Cambridge, Mass.: Harvard University Press, 1954). The work includes a letter to John Hay in which Roosevelt describes much of his ranching experience. Additional letters were found in *Letters from Theodore Roosevelt to Anna Roosevelt Cowles, 1870–1918* (New York: Charles Scribner's Sons, 1924), and in *Letters of Theodore Roosevelt* (Cambridge, Mass.: Harvard University Press, 1951). Roosevelt's own books provided insights, including *Hunting Trips of a Ranchman; Sketches of a Sport on the Northern Cattle Plains* (New York: G. P. Putnam's Sons, 1922); *Ranch Life and Hunting-Trail* (New York: Century Co., n.d. [1888]), which was illustrated by Frederic Remington; and *Theodore Roosevelt, an Autobiography* (New York: Charles Scribner's Sons, 1920).

ABOUT THE AUTHOR

David Dary is a native of Manhattan, Kansas, where his maternal great grandfather settled at the end of the Civil War. His paternal grandfather, born in Canada, homesteaded in Dickinson County, Kansas, in 1873. After graduation from Kansas State University, the author spent nearly fifteen years as a working journalist in Kansas, Texas, and Washington, D.C., where he covered the White House and other government agencies for CBS News during the last weeks of the Eisenhower and then the Kennedy administrations. He then spent four years in management with NBC News in Washington, D.C., during the Johnson administration before returning to Kansas in the late 1960s. He joined the faculty of the William Allen White School of Journalism at the University of Kansas, earned his master's degree, and spent twenty years climbing the ranks to full professor. During this time he began writing first on Kansas and then on the early history of the American West. In 1989, he became head of what is now the Gaylord College of Journalism at the University of Oklahoma. He retired in 2000 after eleven years in that position and has since devoted his time to research and writing on the Old West. He and his wife, Sue, reside in Norman, Oklahoma.

INDEX

237